Cymbeline, The Winter's Tale, and *The Tempest*

An Annotated Bibliography of Shakespeare Studies 1864–2000

Presented to Purchase College
by
Gary Waller, PhD Cambridge

State University of New York
Distinguished Professor

Professor
of Literature & Cultural
Studies, and Theatre &
Performance, 1995-2019
Provost 1995-2004

PEGASUS SHAKESPEARE BIBLIOGRAPHIES
General Editor
RICHARD L. NOCHIMSON
Yeshiva University

Cymbeline, The Winter's Tale, and *The Tempest*

An Annotated Bibliography of Shakespeare Studies
1864–2000

Edited by
JOHN S. MEBANE

Pegasus Press
FAIRVIEW, NC
2002

© Copyright 2002

Pegasus Press

101 BOOTER ROAD
FAIRVIEW, NC 28730

www.pegpress.org

Library of Congress Cataloguing-in-Publication Data

Cymbeline, The winter's tale, and The tempest : an annotated bibliography of
Shakespeare studies, 1864-2000 / edited by John S. Mebane.
    p. cm. — (Pegasus Shakespeare bibliographies)
Includes bibliographical references and indexes.
ISBN 1–889818–31–3
1. Shakespeare, William, 1564-1616. Cymbeline—Bibliography. 2. Shakespeare,
William, 1564-1616. Winter's tale—Bibliography. 3. Shakespeare, William,
1564-1616. Tempest—Bibliography. I. Mebane, John S., 1946– II. Series.
    Z8812.C9 C96 2003
    [PR2806]
    822.3'3—dc21

                                                            2002156425

Cover: A sixteenth-century image of the Golden Age (*The Tempest*, 2.1),
    from Ovid, *Accipe studiose lector ... Metamorphosin* (1509). By permis-
    sion of the Folger Shakespeare Library.

This book has been typeset in Garamond
at Pegasus Press and has been made to last.
It is printed on acid-free paper
to library specifications.

Printed in the United States of America.

CONTENTS

PREFACE

The twelve volumes of this series, of which this is the seventh, are designed to provide a guide to secondary materials on Shakespeare not only for scholars but also for graduate and undergraduate students and for college and high school teachers. In nine of the twelve volumes, entries will refer to materials that focus on individual works by Shakespeare; a total of twenty-five plays, plus *The Rape of Lucrece*, will be covered in these volumes. The remaining three volumes will present materials that treat Shakespeare in more general ways. These are highly selective bibliographies. While making sure to represent different approaches to the study of Shakespeare, the editors are including only work that is either of high quality or of great influence.

In this volume, entries for the works included are numbered consecutively throughout the volume. Within each subsection, entries are organized alphabetically by author.

Each entry contains the basic factual information and an annotation. Since inclusion of an item in this bibliography implies recognition of high quality or significant influence, the annotations are primarily descriptive rather than evaluative. Readers will find that where evaluative comments have been considered helpful to the reader (or irresistible to the editor) they appear at the end of an annotation. Because of the extraordinary cultural influence of these plays—especially *The Tempest*—this volume includes (principally in subsection V G) entries for a number of creative works written in response to Shakespeare, including poetry, fiction, and original films.

Although "romance" and "tragicomedy" are the generic designations most frequently applied to *Cymbeline, The Winter's Tale*, and *The Tempest*, there is significant debate about the genre of these works. The term "late plays" has been adopted in the heading of Section II as the designation most acceptable to the broadest range of scholars and readers. Within individual entries, the editor's choice of terms reflects that of the author whose work is being annotated.

The organization of this volume is as follows.

Section I, which will be essentially the same in all twelve volumes, contains those editions and general reference works that in the collective opinion of the editors are most basic to the study of Shakespeare. The annotations in this section have been written by the following series editors: Jean E. Howard, Clifford C. Huffman, John S. Mebane (who has undertaken the updating as well as the composing of the annotations in subsections A and B), Richard L. Nochimson, Hugh M. Richmond, Barbara H. Traister, and John W. Velz.

Section II is devoted to the late plays as a group; each item in that section discusses at least two, and typically three, plays. Sections III, IV, and V are devoted to *Cymbeline*, *The Winter's Tale*, and *The Tempest*, respectively. Each of these sections is divided into subsections; the table of contents indicates the kinds of works included in each subsection. Many items, of course, cannot be neatly categorized under the heading of a single subsection. When an item could easily fall into more than one subsection, the editor of this volume has placed the item in the most appropriate one, and has cross-referenced it at the end of the other relevant subsections. For example, Barbara Howard Traister's *Heavenly Necromancers: The Magician in English Renaissance Drama* (no. 240) appears in Section V, subsection E ("Criticism"), and it is cross-referenced at the end of subsection V C ("Influences ... "). Readers should consult the cross-references at the end of each subsection, as well as the subject index (where items are listed by item number only), to see the full range of material relevant to a given area or topic. Since all of the items in this bibliography could be considered forms of "criticism," no cross-references are listed at the end of that subsection.

No item in this bibliography is given more than one bibliographical entry. The only exception to this rule involves the entries in Section I for eight especially valuable multi–volume editions of Shakespeare's works, such as the Arden Shakespeare. Where appropriate, volumes from those editions are also described individually in the subsections on "Editions" in Sections III, IV, and V.

Sections II, III, IV, and V include a subsection for "Collections." The items in these subsections include collections of both previously published and original materials. Selected materials in these collections are annotated elsewhere in the volume; these are listed by cross-references in the collection annotations, and the individual entries, in turn, refer to the collection entries. The collection entries often contain brief descriptions of other critical, scholarly, or creative materials that do not receive an independent annotation elsewhere in this bibliography.

The earliest item to receive an independent annotation is Robert Browning's "Caliban upon Setebos," published in 1864. Information concerning criticism or creative works written prior to that date is included in the annotations of the variorum editions and collections in Sections III, IV, and V. Listings for prominent early critics, such as Samuel Johnson and Samuel Taylor Coleridge, mentioned in those annotations appear in Index I.

Within the entries, numbers prefaced by "no." indicate cross-references; numbers in parentheses indicate either the page numbers in the book or article where a specific topic is discussed or quoted, or the act, scene, and line numbers of the passage discussed, divided by periods (e.g., 5.5.45–50). Unless specified otherwise, the act, scene, and line designations are taken from *The Riverside Shakespeare* (no. 2).

Abbreviations used are listed on the next page.

Acknowledgements

Portions of the research for this bibliography were funded by the Minigrant Research Program of the University of Alabama in Huntsville. Expert assistance in the earlier stages of bibliographic searching was provided by Kay Campbell and Bobbie Graham. Final stages of the work were completed during a sabbatical leave provided to the volume editor by the University of Alabama in Huntsville. The editors wish to thank their wives as well as all those colleagues and friends who helped with the compiling of this bibliography.

John S. Mebane
University of Alabama, Huntsville

Richard L. Nochimson
Yeshiva University

December 2000

Abbreviations

cf.	compare
chap., chaps.	chapter(s)
Co.	company
Cym	*Cymbeline*
ed., eds.	edited by/editor(s)
e.g.	for example
et al.	and others
et passim	and in various places
i.e.	that is
no., nos.	number(s)
n.p.	no place given
n.s.	new series
p., pp.	page(s)
repr.	reprint/reprinted
SQ	*Shakespeare Quarterly*
Tmp	*The Tempest*
trans.	translated by
Univ.	University
vol., vols.	volume(s)
WT	*The Winter's Tale*

I. EDITIONS AND REFERENCE WORKS

A. Single-Volume Editions.

1. Bevington, David, ed. *The Complete Works of Shakespeare.* Updated 4th edition. New York: Addison Wesley Longman, 1997.

Bevington's *Complete Works* includes 38 plays and the nondramatic poems. Introductions, aimed at a broad audience, focus upon questions of interpretation. The general introduction discusses social, intellectual, and theatrical history; Shakespeare's biography and his career as a dramatist; his language and versification; editions and editors of Shakespeare; and the history of Shakespearean criticism. Appendices include discussions of canon, dates, and early texts; brief summaries of sources; and performance history. There are genealogical charts, maps, and a selected bibliography. Emendations of the copy text are recorded only in an appendix; they are not bracketed in the texts of the plays. Spelling is modernized unless an exception is necessary for scansion, to indicate a pun, or for other reasons discussed in the preface. Notes appear at the bottom of the column. Speech prefixes are expanded. Illustrations include photographs from recent performances. Features ranging from the clarity and high quality of the introductions to the readability of the typeface combine to make the texts in this edition admirably accessible to students and general readers. Available with this edition are the BBC's CD-ROM programs on *Macbeth* and *A Midsummer Night's Dream.* These multimedia resources provide the full text and complete audio recordings; footnotes; word and image searches; sources; comments and audio-visual aids on plot, themes, language, performance history, historical background, and characterization; print capability; and clips from film and video performances. A *Teacher's Guide* to the CD provides suggestions for assignments and classroom use.

2. Evans, G. Blakemore, et al., eds. *The Riverside Shakespeare.* 2nd edition. Boston: Houghton Mifflin, 1997.

This edition includes 39 plays, the nondramatic poems, and segments of *Sir Thomas More.* Introductions by Herschel Baker (histories), Frank Kermode (tragedies), Hallett Smith (romances and nondramatic poems), Anne Barton (comedies), and J. J. M. Tobin ("A Funeral Elegy" by W. S.

and *Edward III*) discuss dates, sources, and major interpretive issues. Harry Levin's general introduction discusses Shakespeare's biography, artistic development, and reputation; intellectual backgrounds; Renaissance playhouses and theatrical conventions; Elizabethan English; and stylistic techniques. Heather Dubrow provides an analytical survey of twentieth-century Shakespeare criticism. Evans provides an introduction to textual criticism. Appendices include a history of Shakespearean performance by Charles H. Shattuck and William T. Liston; substantial excerpts from historical documents related to Shakespeare's life and works, including some early responses to the plays; "Annals, 1552–1616," a listing in four parallel columns of events in political history, Shakespeare's biography, theater history, and nondramatic literature; a selected bibliography; indexes; and a glossary. Emendations of the copy text are enclosed in square brackets, and each play is followed by a summary discussion of editorial problems and by textual notes listing the sources of all emendations. Spelling is modernized except for "a selection of Elizabethan spelling forms that reflect ... contemporary pronunciation" (67). Notes appear at the bottom of the column. The volume includes numerous illustrations, including color plates. While the *Riverside* has many features aimed at general readers, the impressive textual apparatus, Evans's fine discussion of textual criticism, and the collection of documents make this edition of special interest to advanced graduate students and to scholars.

3. Greenblatt, Stephen, Walter Cohen, Jean E. Howard, and Katharine Eisaman Maus, eds. *The Norton Shakespeare, Based on the Oxford Edition*. New York: Norton, 1997.

This edition includes 38 plays (including quarto, folio, and conflated texts of *King Lear*) and the nondramatic poems, including works of uncertain authorship not included in other single-volume editions. The texts (except for "A Funeral Elegy," ed. Donald Foster) are updated versions of those in the modern-spelling, single-volume *Oxford Shakespeare* (1988) produced by general editors Stanley Wells and Gary Taylor with John Jowett and William Montgomery. The *Oxford* edition is based on revisionary editorial principles, including the belief that some texts previously regarded as having limited authority are in reality records (at times highly imperfect) of early authorial versions later revised in the theater. The revised versions are usually chosen as control texts. In the *Oxford*, passages from earlier versions are often reprinted in appendices; the *Norton* prints these passages from earlier versions, indented, within the texts. *The Norton Shakespeare* provides marginal glosses and numerous explanatory notes; the latter are numbered in the text and appear at the bottom of each page. Textual variants are listed after each work. Stage directions added after the 1623 Folio appear in brackets. Greenblatt's general introduction discusses Renaissance economic, social, religious, and political life; Shakespeare's biography; textual criticism; and aspects of Shakespeare's art, including "The Paradoxes of Identity" in characterization and analysis of the "overpowering exuberance and generosity" (63) of Shakespeare's language. Introductions to individual works discuss a range of historical and aesthetic issues. Appendices include Andrew Gurr's "The Shakespearean Stage"; a collection of documents; a chronicle of events in political and literary history; a bibliography; and a glossary. This edition combines traditional scholarship with a focus on such recent concerns as the status of women and "The English and Otherness." Also available is *The Norton Shakespeare Workshop*, ed. Mark Rose, a set of interactive multimedia programs on CD-ROM that can be purchased either separately or in a package with *The Norton Shakespeare*. The *Workshop* provides searchable texts of *A Midsummer Night's Dream*; *The Merchant of Venice*; *Henry IV, Part Two*; *Othello*; *Hamlet*; *The Tempest*; and Sonnets 55 and 138. Students can find analyses of selected passages, sources, essays that illustrate the play's critical and performance history, clips from classic and from specially commissioned performances, selections of music inspired by the plays, and tools for developing paper topics.

4. Hinman, Charlton, ed. *The Norton Facsimile: The First Folio of Shakespeare*. 2nd edition. Introduction by Peter Blayney. New York: W. W. Norton, 1996.

The First Folio of 1623 is a collection of 36 plays made by Shakespeare's fellow actors, Heminge and Condell. *Pericles, The Two Noble Kinsmen*, and the nondramatic poems are not included. Heminge and Condell claim to have provided "perfect" texts, distinguishing them from what they describe as "stolne, and surreptitious copies, maimed, and deformed by the frauds and stealthes of injurious impostors" (A3). While some of the previously published quartos are regarded today as superior versions, the First Folio indeed provides the most authoritative texts for the majority of Shakespeare's plays. It also includes commendatory poems by four authors, including Ben Jonson, and the Droeshout portrait of Shakespeare. During the two years that the 1623 edition was in press, corrections were made continually, and the uncorrected pages became mingled with corrected ones. In addition, imperfections of various sorts render portions of numerous pages difficult or impossible to read. Hinman has examined the 80 copies of the First Folio in the Folger Shakespeare Library and selected the clearest versions of what appear to be the finally corrected pages. In the left and right margins, he provides for reference his system of "through line numbering," by which he numbers each typographical line throughout the text of a play (the verse and prose of the play as well as all other material such as scene headings and stage directions). In a page from *King John*, for example, which includes what might otherwise be referred to as 3.1.324 through 3.3.74 (this form of reference appears in the bottom margin), the through line numbers run from 1257 to 1380. Appendix A presents some variant states of the Folio text, and Appendix B lists the Folger copies used in compiling this edition. Hinman's introduction discusses the nature and authority of the Folio, the printing and proofreading process, and the procedures followed in editing the facsimile, explaining, among other points, the advantages of through line numbering. Blayney's introduction updates Hinman's discussions of such matters as the status of quarto texts, the types of play-manuscripts available to printers, and the printing and proofreading processes. Blayney also discusses the theory that, since different versions of a given play may represent authorial or collaborative revisions, in such cases there is no "ideal text." No interpretive introductions or glosses are provided. While some valuable facsimiles of quarto versions are available, the Hinman First Folio is clearly an excellent place to begin one's encounter with early printed texts that are not mediated by centuries of editorial tradition.

B. Multi-Volume Editions.

5. Barnet, Sylvan, general ed. *The Signet Classic Shakespeare*. New York: Penguin.

Originally edited in the 1960s, the Signet series was updated in the 1980s; newly revised volumes began to appear in 1998. The 35–volume series includes 38 plays and the nondramatic poems. Collections entitled *Four Great Comedies, Four Great Tragedies*, and *The Sonnets and Nondramatic Poems* are available. Each volume in the newly revised series includes a general introduction with discussions of Shakespeare's biography, including the "anti-Stratfordian" authorship phenomenon; Shakespeare's English; Elizabethan theaters; "Shakespeare's Dramatic Language: Costumes, Gestures and Silences; Prose and Poetry"; editorial principles; and the staging of Shakespeare's plays, including consideration of the concept of the play as a collaboration among the playwright, theatrical ensemble, and audience. Spelling is generally modernized, and speech prefixes are expanded. Explanatory notes appear at the bottom of each page. Appendices contain textual notes, discussion of (and often excerpts from) sources, several critical essays, a survey of each play's performance history, and a bibliography. Although introductions in this series are written for beginning students, the substantial selection of distinguished critical essays is useful for more advanced students, as well.

6. Bevington, David, ed. David Scott Kastan, James Hammersmith, and Robert Kean Turner, associate eds. *The Bantam Shakespeare*. New York: Bantam, 1988.

In 1988, 37 plays and the nondramatic poems were published in the 29 volumes of *The Bantam Shakespeare*. Collections entitled *Four Comedies* and *Four Tragedies* are available. Texts, explanatory notes (at the bottom of each page), and interpretive introductions are similar to those of Bevington's *Complete Works of Shakespeare* (see no. 1). Included in the Bantam series are brief performance histories of individual plays and Joseph Papp's forewords on Shakespeare's enduring appeal. Each volume includes a one-page biography of Shakespeare and an introduction to Elizabethan playhouses. Appendices include concise discussions of dates and early texts, textual notes, substantial excerpts from sources, and a brief annotated bibliography. While this series necessarily excludes some of the historical information found in the *Complete Works*, the forewords by an eminent producer/director and the well-written performance histories are engaging features, especially appropriate for students and general readers.

7. Brockbank, Philip, founding general ed. Brian Gibbons, general ed. A. R. Braunmuller, associate general ed. *The New Cambridge Shakespeare*. Cambridge: Cambridge Univ. Press, 1982—.

The New Cambridge series will eventually include 39 plays (with *The Reign of Edward III*) and the nondramatic poems. So far, 41 volumes have appeared; among these are two separate editions (one based on an early quarto) of *King Lear*, of *Hamlet*, of *Richard III*, and of *Henry V*. Introductions discuss date, sources, critical history and interpretive issues, staging, and performance history (with numerous illustrations). Discussion of the text precedes each play, and more detailed textual analysis sometimes appears in an appendix. All volumes include a selected bibliography. Spelling is generally modernized; speech prefixes are expanded. Textual notes signaling departures from the copy text and extensive explanatory notes appear at the bottom of each page. Designed for students and scholars, *The New Cambridge Shakespeare* provides more detailed attention to stagecraft and performance history than most other editions. This series succeeds *The New Shakespeare*, edited by Arthur Quiller-Couch and John Dover Wilson.

8. Knowles, Richard, and Paul Werstine, general eds. Robert K. Turner, senior consulting editor. *A New Variorum Edition of Shakespeare*. New York: Modern Language Association.

From 1871 to 1928 H. H. Furness, Sr., and H. H. Furness, Jr., published

19 works of the Variorum Shakespeare. Since 1933, nine new editions have appeared in the MLA series. The completed 40–volume variorum will contain 38 plays and the nondramatic poems. Each volume provides an old-spelling text and a collation of significant emendations from previous editions. Explanatory notes (printed below the textual notes at the bottom of each page) try to record all important previous annotation. Appendices include discussions of a play's text and date. Recent volumes survey the history of criticism and performance and refer to a substantial bibliography; early volumes include excerpts from previous criticism. Sources and analogues are discussed and reprinted. As compilations of scholarship, criticism, and textual analysis, these volumes represent a significant resource for scholars and teachers.

9. Mowat, Barbara A., and Paul Werstine, eds. *The New Folger Library Shakespeare.* New York: Pocket Books, Washington Square Press, 1992—.

Twenty-seven volumes of the New Folger series, which replaces *The Folger Library General Reader's Shakespeare*, appeared between 1992 and 2002. Several new titles will come out each year until the series of 38 plays and the nondramatic poems is complete. Each volume provides a brief initial comment on the play followed by basic introductions to Shakespeare's language and style, his biography, Elizabethan theaters, early editions, and the editorial principles of the series. Half brackets enclose emendations of the copy text; in some volumes square or pointed brackets indicate the sources of passages that appear (for example) only in the folio or an earlier quarto. Explanatory notes appear on pages facing the text, textual notes in an appendix. Spelling is selectively modernized, and speech prefixes are expanded. For each play a different critic offers the "Modern Perspective" that follows the text. A brief annotated bibliography focuses mostly on recent approaches to the play; standard works on language, biography, theatrical setting, and early texts also appear. While this series aims at the broadest possible audience, the clarity and helpfulness of its introductions and explanatory notes make it especially well suited for beginning students.

10. Proudfoot, Richard, Ann Thompson, and David Scott Kastan, general eds. *The Arden Shakespeare.* Walton-on-Thames, Surrey: Nelson House.

The 40–volume *Arden Shakespeare* includes 38 plays and 2 volumes of the nondramatic poems. The edition is continually updated; although some current volumes are from the 1950s, thirteen plays and the Sonnets have appeared in revised third editions in recent years. Introductions provide extensive discussion of dates, texts, editorial principles, sources, and a wide range of interpretive issues. Extensive textual and explanatory notes appear at the bottom of each page. Appendices typically include additional textual analysis, excerpts from sources, and (sometimes) settings for songs. The Arden series often includes scholarship and criticism that are essential for advanced students and scholars. The complete second edition of the Arden series is available on CD-ROM from Primary Source Media. The CD-ROMs enable one to view the edited texts simultaneously with materials from the following: early quarto and folio editions; Bullough's *Narrative and Dramatic Sources* (no. 15); Abbott's *Shakespearian Grammar*; Onions's *Shakespeare Glossary* (no. 23); Partridge's *Shakespeare's Bawdy*; and a 4,600–item bibliography. The complete Arden set is also available on-line, with additional materials for those works that have appeared in the third edition.

11. Spencer, T. J. B., founding general ed. Stanley Wells, associate ed. *The New Penguin Shakespeare*. London: Penguin Books.

The 40–volume New Penguin series now includes 37 plays and the nondramatic poems; *Cymbeline* is planned. Dates range from the 1960s through 2001. Introductions discuss a range of interpretive issues and are followed by brief bibliographical essays. Explanatory notes follow the text, succeeded by textual analysis, selective textual notes, and (as appropriate) settings for songs. Spelling is modernized, and speech prefixes are expanded. Emendations of the copy text are not bracketed. The New Penguin will appeal especially to those who wish the pages of the text to be free of annotation.

12. Wells, Stanley, general ed. Advisory eds. S. Schoenbaum, G. R. Proudfoot, and F. W. Sternfeld. *The Oxford Shakespeare*. Oxford: Oxford Univ. Press.

Between 1982 and 2002, 27 plays and *Shakespeare: The Complete Sonnets and Poems* were published in the multi–volume *Oxford Shakespeare*. The completed series will include 38 plays and the nondramatic poems. Introductions provide detailed discussion of dates, sources, textual criticism, questions of interpretation, and performance history. Textual notes and extensive commentary appear at the bottom of each page. The commentary and introduction are indexed. Spelling is modernized, and speech prefixes are expanded. The Oxford series is based on revisionary editorial principles, including the belief that some texts previously regarded as of little value are in reality records (at times highly imperfect) of early authorial versions later revised in the theater. The revised versions are usually chosen as copy texts, and appendices sometimes include passages from earlier printed versions. Some appendices include musical settings for songs. Partly because of its editorial principles, this series is of special interest to scholars and advanced students.

C. Basic Reference Works for Shakespeare Studies.

13. Beckerman, Bernard. *Shakespeare at the Globe: 1599–1609.* New York: Macmillan, 1962.

This study of the 29 extant plays (including 15 by Shakespeare) produced at the Globe in its first decade yields information about the playhouse and how Shakespeare's company performed in it. The first chapter, on the repertory system, is based on analysis of Henslowe's diary. Subsequent chapters about the stage itself, acting styles, the dramatic form of plays and of scenes within plays, and the staging derive from study of the Globe repertory. Detailed appendices provide statistics on which Beckerman's analysis partly depends. Beckerman concludes that the style in which these plays were presented was neither symbolic nor what modern audiences would call realistic. Rather, he suggests, passion by the actors was presented within a framework of staging and scenic conventions in various styles according to the needs of particular plays.

14. Bentley, G. E. *The Jacobean and Caroline Stage.* 7 vols. Oxford: Clarendon Press, 1941–68.

Bentley designed his survey of British drama to carry on that of Chambers (see no. 16) and cover the years 1616–42. The 11 chapters in vol. 1 provide detailed information about 11 adult and children's acting companies (1–342); vol. 2 surveys information about actors, listed alphabetically (343–629), with relevant documents reprinted and annotated (630–96), with an index (697–748). Vols. 3, 4, 5 are an alphabetical list, by author, with bibliographical material and commentary, of "all plays, masques, shows, and dramatic entertainments which were written or first performed in England between 1616 ... and ... 1642" (3.v), from "M.A." to Richard Zouche, with a final section (5. 1281–1456) on anonymous and untitled plays. Vol. 6 considers theater buildings (private, 3–117; public, 121–252; court, 255–88; and two that were only projected, 291–309). Vol. 7 gathers together, as appendices to vol. 6, "scattered material concerning Lenten performances and Sunday performances" and arranges chronologically "a large number of dramatic and semi-dramatic events" of interest to students of dramatic literature and theater history (6.v); it includes a general index for vols. 1–7 (129–390), which has numerous references (344–45) to Shakespeare and his plays.

15. Bullough, Geoffrey. *Narrative and Dramatic Sources of Shakespeare.* 8 vols. London and New York: Routledge and Kegan Paul and Columbia Univ. Press, 1957–75.

This work is a comprehensive compendium of the texts of Shakespeare's sources for 37 plays and several poems. Bullough includes analogues as well as sources and "possible sources" as well as "probable sources." All texts are in English, old-spelling Elizabethan when extant, and in some other cases in the compiler's translation. Bullough includes a separate introduction for each play. In the early volumes, interpretation is largely left to the reader; introductions in the later volumes include more interpretation and tend to be longer. There have been complaints of occasional errors in transcription. The major caveat, however, about using this learned, thorough, and imaginative work concerns what Bullough could not conceivably print: the passages in his sources that Shakespeare presumably read but either chose to omit or neglected to include.

16. Chambers, E. K. *The Elizabethan Stage.* 4 vols. Oxford: Clarendon Press, 1923. Revised 1945; with corrections 1967.

In vol. 1, Chambers provides detailed information about the court (1–234): the monarchs, their households, the Revels Office, pageantry, the mask, and the court play. In the section entitled "The Control of the Stage" (236–388), he covers the struggles between the city of London and the court and between Humanism and Puritanism, and treats the status of actors and the socio-economic realities of actors' lives. In vol. 2, Chambers focuses on the history of 38 different acting companies (children, adult, and foreign) (1–294), gives details, such as are known, about an alphabetical list of actors (295–350), and treats the playhouses (16 public and 2 private theaters), including discussion of their structure and management (351–557). In vol. 3, Chambers surveys the conditions of staging in the court and theaters (1–154), the printing of plays (157–200), and then offers a bibliographical survey, including brief biographies, of playwrights alphabetically arranged, from William Alabaster through Christopher Yelverton (201–518). In vol. 4, Chambers concludes that bibliography with anonymous work (1–74) and presents 13 appendices that reprint or summarize relevant historical documents. Chambers concludes this work with four indices (to plays, persons, places, and subjects) to the four volumes (409–67). In these four volumes, Chambers presents an encyclopedia of all aspects of English drama during the reigns of Elizabeth I and James I up to the date of Shakespeare's death in 1616. A subsequent and detailed index to this entire work was compiled by Beatrice White, *An Index to "The Elizabethan Stage" and "William Shakespeare" by Sir Edmund Chambers.* Oxford: Oxford Univ. Press, 1934.

17. Chambers, E. K. *William Shakespeare: A Study of Facts and Problems.* 2 vols. Oxford: Clarendon Press, 1930. Repr., 1931.

This work is an encyclopedia of information relating to Shakespeare.

The principal topics of the first volume are the dramatist's family origins, his relations to the theater and its professionals, the nature of the texts of his plays—including their preparation for performance and publication, and also questions of authenticity and chronology (relevant tables about the quartos and metrics are in the second volume). The data available (and plausible conjectures) concerning all texts attributed to Shakespeare, including poems and uncertain attributions, are then laid out title by title. The second volume cites the significant Shakespeare records then available, including contemporary allusions, performance data, legends, and even forgeries (the last two items are more fully covered in Schoenbaum's *Shakespeare's Lives*). There are comprehensive indices and a substantial bibliography. While it is sometimes necessary to update this book by correlation with Schoenbaum's *Documentary Life* (see no. 25) and other, more recent, texts, Chambers's scholarship has been supplemented rather than invalidated by more recent research, and his work remains a convenient starting point for pursuit of background data on Shakespeare's life and works.

18. De Grazia, Margreta, and Stanley Wells, eds. *The Cambridge Companion to Shakespeare*. Cambridge: Cambridge Univ. Press, 2001.

Following a preface, a "partial chronology" of Shakespeare's life and a "conjectural" one of his works, the nineteen chapters of this new edition of the *Cambridge Companion* (the others were 1934, 1971, and 1986) provide a "broadly historical or cultural approach" instead of the earlier volumes' "formalist orientation" (xv). Ernst Honigmann writes on Shakespeare's life (chap. 1), Barbara A. Mowat discusses the traditions of editing (chap. 2, an essay supplemented by Michael Dobson's survey of page- or stage-oriented editions, chap. 15), Leonard Barkan reviews what Shakespeare read (chap. 3), and Margreta De Grazia skims over some aspects of language and rhetoric (chap. 4). John Kerrigan is specific in his discussion of the poems (chap. 5), a specificity balanced by the more general essays of Susan Snyder on the possibilities of genre (chap. 6), Valerie Traub on Shakespeare's use of gender and sexuality (chap. 9), and David Scott Kastan on the use of history (chap. 11). Social background—the City, Court, Playhouse, etc.—are the subjects of chapters by John H. Astington and Anne Barton (chaps. 7, 8), and Ania Loomba goes farther afield in spotlighting "outsiders" in England and Shakespeare (chap. 10). The last chapters group into two divisions: Shakespeare's posthumous presence in the (British) theater of 1660–1900 (Lois Potter, chap. 12) and in that of the 20th century (Peter Holland, chap. 13), in the cinema (Russell Jackson, chap. 14), on stages and pages worldwide (Dennis Kennedy, chap. 16); and, second, the history of Shakespeare criticism (1600–1900 by Hugh Grady, chap. 17; 1900–2000 by

R. S. White, chap. 18). The volume concludes with an annotated list of Shakespeare reference books recommended by Dieter Mehl (chap. 19). Each essay except the last appends its own (further) reading list.

This volume does not precisely replace its immediate predecessor (ed. Wells, 1986, repr. 1991), for the latter's "basic materials ... on Shakespeare's life, ... the transmission of the text, and the history of both criticism and production are still [fortunately] available" (xvi). This availability does not prevent the present volume from printing new essays on some of the same topics; and students, teachers, and scholars may well benefit from comparing the generations—for instance Ernst Honigmann with S. Schoenbaum on Shakespeare's biography, Margreta De Grazia with Inga-Stina Ewbank on Shakespeare and language, Russell Jackson with Robert Hapgood on film (and, in the earlier edition, television) versions of Shakespeare, Hugh Grady with Harry Levin on Shakespeare criticism to about 1900, and R. S. White with the three scholars who wrote three separate essays on his topic, 20th-century Shakespeare criticism. The 1986 edition, then, should be consulted in addition to this new entry.

19. Doran, Madeleine. *Endeavors of Art: A Study of Form in Elizabethan Drama.* Madison: Univ. of Wisconsin Press, 1954.

Doran reconstructs the Elizabethan assumptions about many aspects of dramatic form, defined broadly enough to include genre, eloquence and copiousness, character, and "moral aim." A detailed exploration of classical, medieval, and Renaissance backgrounds makes this a study in historical criticism; however, the cultural context laid out is aesthetic, not ideational. Doran examines the problems of form faced by Shakespeare and his contemporaries—problems of genre, of character, of plot construction—in an attempt to explain the success (or, sometimes, lack of success) of the major dramatists in "achieving form adequate to meaning" (23). Doran's unpretentious, readable study is justly famous as the first book on the aesthetics of Renaissance drama to understand the entire context, to perceive the Renaissance assumptions about dramatic art as a fusion of classical and medieval influences.

20. Gurr, Andrew. *Playgoing in Shakespeare's London.* 2nd edition. Cambridge: Cambridge Univ. Press, 1996.

Gurr focuses on the identity, class, and changing tastes of London playgoers from the opening of the Red Lion in 1567 to the closing of the theaters in 1642. He examines the locations, physical features, price scales, and repertories of the various playhouses, distinguishing particularly between "halls" and "amphitheatres" and rejecting the more common labels "private" and "public." Turning from the theaters, Gurr examines the playgoers, asking

such questions as whether they ventured to the playhouses primarily to
"hear" a text or to "see" a spectacle. In a final chapter, entitled "The evolution of tastes," he discusses assorted playgoing fashions: from the craze
for Tarlton's clowning to the taste for pastoral and romance in the last
years of Charles I. Two appendices list identifiable playgoers and references to playgoing during the time period.

21. Gurr, Andrew. *The Shakespearean Stage 1574–1642*. 3rd edition. Cambridge: Cambridge Univ. Press, 1992.

Gurr summarizes a vast amount of scholarship concerning the material conditions of Elizabethan, Jacobean, and Caroline theatrical production. Each of his six chapters provides a wealth of detailed information on
theatrical life. The first gives an overview of the place of the theater in
urban London from the 1570s until 1642, including an examination of the
social status of playwrights, the differences and similarities between the
repertories at the open-air amphitheaters (public) and at the indoor
playhouses (private), and the changing role of court patronage of theater.
Chapter 2 describes the typical composition of London theater companies
and their regulation by the Crown. It also gives an historical account of
the theatrical companies that at various times dominated the London
theatrical scene. In his third chapter, Gurr looks at actors, discussing the
famous clowns of the Elizabethan era, prominent tragic actors such as
Burbage and Alleyn, and the repertory system within which they worked.
The fourth chapter summarizes what is known about the playhouses,
including information gleaned from the recent excavation of the remains
of the Rose Theater, as well as accounts of the Globe Theater, The Fortune, the hall playhouses, and the Banqueting Hall. Chapter 5 discusses
staging conventions and the differences between public and private theaters,
and among the various particular theaters, in their use of song, music,
clowning, and jigging. Also examined are stage properties and costumes.
The final chapter analyzes information about audiences: who went to which
kinds of playhouse and how they behaved. Gurr argues that women and
all social classes were represented in theatrical audiences, with an increasing tendency in the seventeenth century for the private theaters to cater
to a wealthier clientele who demanded a more sophisticated repertory with
more new plays. This valuable book concludes with an appendix indicating
at which playhouses and by which companies various plays were staged.

22. Kastan, David Scott, ed. *A Companion to Shakespeare*. Oxford: Black-
well Publishers, 1999.

This collection of 28 essays, most with notes and references for further reading, aims to locate Shakespeare in relation to the historical matrix in which he wrote his plays and poems. Following the editor's introduction, the volume is framed by two essays dealing with Shakespeare the man. The first, by David Bevington, deals with what is known, factually, about his life; the last, by Michael Bristol, deals with various myths surrounding the figure of Shakespeare. In between, the book is divided into five sections. The first contains six essays, mainly by historians, dealing with Shakespeare's England, the city of London, religious identities of the period, the family and household structures, Shakespeare and political thought, and the political culture of the Tudor-Stuart period. The second section contains five essays, mostly by literary critics, and discusses readers and reading practices in the early modern period. It includes a general essay on literacy, illiteracy, and reading practices, and four essays focusing on reading, respectively, the Bible, the classics, historical writings, and vernacular literature. The third part of the book deals with writing and writing practices and contains five essays by literary scholars on writing plays, on the state of the English language in Shakespeare's day, on technical aspects of Shakespeare's dramatic verse, on the rhetorical culture of the times, and on genre. These essays are followed by a section on playing and performance. It contains five essays, mostly by theater historians, on the economics of playing, on The Chamberlain's-King's Men, on Shakespeare's repertory, on playhouses of the day, and on licensing and censorship. The final section, consisting of five essays by literary critics, deals with aspects of printing and print culture, including Shakespeare's works in print between 1593 and 1640, manuscript playbooks, the craft of printing, the London book trade, and press censorship. Mixing traditional and newer topics and concerns, *A Companion to Shakespeare* is an up-to-date guide to the historical conditions and the literary and theatrical resources enabling Shakespeare's art.

23. Onions, C. T. *A Shakespeare Glossary.* Oxford: Clarendon Press, 1911. 2nd edition revised, 1919. Repr., with corrections, 1946; with enlarged Addenda, 1958. Enlarged and revised by Robert D. Eagleson, 1986; corrected, 1988.

Onions's dictionary of Elizabethan vocabulary as it applies to Shakespeare was an offshoot of his work on the *Oxford English Dictionary.* Eagleson updates the third edition with new entries, using modern research (now aided by citations from the Riverside edition [see no. 2], keyed by the Spevack *Concordance* [see no. 26]), while conserving much from Onions's adaptation of *OED* entries to distinguish Shakespearean uses from those of his contemporaries and from modern standard meanings.

The glossary covers only expressions that differ from modern usage, as with "cousin" or "noise." It includes some proper names with distinctive associations, such as "Machiavel," and explains unfamiliar stage directions: "sennet" (a trumpet signal). Many allusions are more fully elucidated, as with the origin of "hobby-horse" in morris dances, or the bearing of "wayward" on *Macbeth*'s "weird sisters." This text, which demonstrates the importance of historical awareness of language for accuracy in the close reading of Shakespeare, now has a brief bibliography of relevant texts. It still needs to be supplemented in two areas: information about definite and possible sexual significance of many common and obscure words appears in Gordon Williams's 3–volume *A Dictionary of Sexual Language and Imagery in Shakespearean and Stuart Literature* (1994); often contradictory guidance about the likely pronunciation of Shakespeare's language is provided by Helge Kökeritz's *Shakespeare's Pronunciation* (1953) and by Fausto Cercignani's *Shakespeare's Works and Elizabethan Pronunciation* (1981).

24. Rothwell, Kenneth S., and Annabelle Henkin Melzer. *Shakespeare on Screen: An International Filmography and Videography.* New York: Neal-Schuman, 1990.

This list of film and video versions of Shakespeare seeks to be comprehensive, covering the years 1899–1989, except that it excludes most silent films, referring the reader to Robert Hamilton Ball's *Shakespeare on Silent Film* (1968). It does include "modernizations, spinoffs, musical and dance versions, abridgements, travesties and excerpts" (x). The introduction, by Rothwell, offers an overview of screen versions of Shakespeare (1–17). The body of the work, with over 675 entries (21–316), is organized by play, listed alphabetically, and within each play chronologically. Represented are 37 plays and the *Sonnets*. *Pericles* and *Timon of Athens* appear only in the BBC versions in "The Shakespeare Plays" series. For *Hamlet* we have 87 entries. Included also are another 74 entries (317–35) for documentaries and other "unclassifiable" films and videos that present Shakespeare in some form, such as John Barton's "Playing Shakespeare" series and James Ivory's film, *Shakespeare Wallah*. The sometimes quite extensive entries include information about and evaluation of the production, and an attempt to provide information about distribution and availability. The work concludes with a useful selected bibliography with brief annotations (337–45), a series of helpful indices (349–98), and a list of the names and addresses of distributors, dealers, and archives (399–404).

25. Schoenbaum, S. *William Shakespeare: A Compact Documentary Life.* Oxford: Oxford Univ. Press, 1977. Repr., with corrections, 1978.

An abridged version of Schoenbaum's massive documentary study of Shakespeare published by Oxford in 1975, the *Compact Documentary Life* traces all textual evidence about Shakespeare chronologically from his grandfather's generation up to the deaths of Shakespeare's surviving family members. Legends for which there is no specific documentation—such as the deer-poaching incident—are examined for probability on the basis of surviving materials. Where appropriate, Schoenbaum juxtaposes biographical details with specific passages in Shakespeare's works. Amply illustrated and annotated, this work, unlike Schoenbaum's earlier, larger version and his later (1981) *William Shakespeare: Records and Images*, refers to documents but generally does not reprint them.

26. Spevack, Marvin. *The Harvard Concordance to Shakespeare.* Cambridge: Belknap Press of Harvard Univ. Press, 1973.

This text covers the total of 29,066 words (including proper names) used by Shakespeare in his plays and poems, in the modern-spelling text of *The Riverside Shakespeare* (see no. 2). Stage directions appear in another volume. Contexts are omitted for the first 43 words in order of frequency, mostly pronouns, prepositions, conjunctions, auxiliary verbs, and articles. Individual entries distinguish between prose and verse, and between total and relative frequencies. The modern spelling is not enforced with proper names or significant Elizabethan divergencies: "embassador-ambassador." While the cited context of each use is normally the line of text in which it appears, other limits occur when the sense requires further wording. This concordance helps to locate specific passages and also invites subtler research uses, such as study of the recurrence of words in each play: thus the continuity of *Henry VIII* from *Richard III* appears in their shared distinctive use of certain religious terms. Similarly, accumulated references show the divergence or consistency of meaning or associations for particular terms (Shakespeare's references to dogs are unfavorable). In using this text, one must remember that variant spellings or forms of speech may conceal recurrences of words with the same root or meaning (guilt, gilt, guilts, guilty, guiltily, guiltless), while similar spellings of the same word may have contrasting senses (your grace [the Duke] of York, the grace of God, external grace). The provided contexts reveal the complications, but often are too brief to ensure exact interpretation of a word. The magnitude of the effort involved in this concordance indicates the research gain from electronic procedures, which also permit many permutations of its data, as seen in the nine volumes of Spevack's *A Complete and Systematic Concordance to the Works of Shakespeare* (1968-80).

27. Styan, J. L. *Shakespeare's Stagecraft.* Cambridge: Cambridge Univ. Press, 1967. Repr., with corrections, 1971.

Styan's book explores how Shakespeare's plays would have worked, theatrically, on the Elizabethan stage. Beginning with a discussion of the kind of stage for which Shakespeare wrote and of the conventions of performance that obtained on that stage, Styan then devotes the bulk of his attention to Shakespeare's handling of the visual and aural dimensions of performance. He argues that the scripts guide actors in communicating aurally, visually, and kinetically with an audience. Topics considered include gesture, entrances and exits, the use of downstage and upstage playing areas, eavesdropping encounters, the visual orchestration of scenes involving one or several or many characters, the manipulation of rhythm and tempo, and variations among stage voices. The final chapter, "Total Theater," discusses the inseparability of all the elements of Shakespeare's stagecraft in the shaping of a theatrical event aimed at provoking and engaging the audience's fullest response. The book makes a strong case for studying Shakespeare's plays as flexible blueprints for performance that skillfully utilize and transform the stagecraft conventions of the Elizabethan theater.

Note on Bibliographies

In addition to the above works, readers should be aware of the various bibliographies of Shakespeare studies. Among the most valuable are Stanley Wells, *Shakespeare: A Bibliographical Guide*, Oxford: Clarendon Press, 1990; David M. Bergeron and Geraldo U. De Sousa, *Shakespeare: A Study and Research Guide*, 3rd edition, Lawrence: Univ. Press of Kansas, 1995; Larry S. Champion, *The Essential Shakespeare: An Annotated Bibliography of Major Modern Studies*, 2nd edition, New York: Hall, 1993. Thorough bibliographies for each of a gradually increasing number of plays have been appearing since 1980 in the Garland Shakespeare Bibliographies, general editor William L. Godshalk. An important specialized bibliography is John W. Velz, *Shakespeare and the Classical Tradition: A Critical Guide to Commentary, 1660–1960*, Minneapolis: Univ. of Minnesota Press, 1968 (available on-line). In the special area of Shakespearean pedagogy, a useful (although brief) bibliography appears in Peggy O'Brien, "'And Gladly Teach': Books, Articles, and a Bibliography on the Teaching of Shakespeare," *Shakespeare Quarterly* 46 (1995): 165–72. For information on new materials on the study of Shakespeare, readers should consult the annual bibliographies published by *Shakespeare Quarterly* (*World Shakespeare Bibliography*, also available on line), *PMLA* (*The MLA International Bibliography*, also available on-line and on CD ROM), the Modern Humanities Research Association (*Annual Bibliography of English Language and Literature*, available on-line), and the English Association (*The Year's Work in English Studies*). Ph.D. theses on Shakespeare are listed in *Dissertation Abstracts International*, which is also available on-line.

II. THE LATE PLAYS AS A GROUP

A. Influences; Sources; Intertextuality; Historical and Intellectual Contexts; Topicality.

28. Bate, Jonathan. "From Myth to Drama." Chap. 6 of *Shakespeare and Ovid*, 215–70. Oxford: Clarendon Press, 1993.

This chapter analyzes Shakespeare's transformation of Ovidian materials in the romances. The section on *Cym* (215–19) argues that Shakespeare creates a sense of wonder through anthropomorphic treatment of nature while going beyond Ovid in suggesting the psychological interpretations of myth: Shakespeare interprets the myth of Actaeon, for example, as suggesting that "it is a form of violation to gaze with desire on a woman when she is in a vulnerable state" (218). In the section on *WT* (219–39) Bate emphasizes that "To read mythically is to put every phenomenon sub specie aeternitatis" (227). He thus interprets the bear in 3.3 as an instance of the gods' intervening in human affairs through natural forces. Yet the statue scene (5.3), Bate believes, transforms the myth of Pygmalion by emphasizing human love and forgiveness, rather than magical intervention of the gods. The section on *Tmp* (239–63) argues against the centrality of imperial themes and in favor of Ovidian influences. For Bate, Medea's black magic is invoked so that Prospero can reject it. He concludes that *Tmp* suggests that the Ovidian golden age invoked by Gonzalo is irretrievably lost, yet Prospero's masque provides a vision of the silver age, a time in which law, fruitful labor, and marriage ameliorate the hardships and dangers of the fallen world.

29. Bergeron, David M. *Shakespeare's Romances and the Royal Family.* Lawrence: Univ. Press of Kansas, 1985.

Chap. 1 of this study (1–25) emphasizes that Bergeron explores not "one-to-one identifications" (25) between literary characters and historical persons, but rather the manner in which Shakespeare read the royal family as a text that he then transformed as he did other sources. In chap. 2 (27–72), Bergeron discusses the personalities and relationships of James's family, with emphasis on the "hope of political and moral renewal" (71) through children, despite the presence of conflict and corruption. Chap.

3 (73–112) surveys treatments of the family in Jacobean comedy, contrasting the emphasis on greed, lust, jealousy, and contests for dominance in satirical plays about commoners with the affirmation of forgiveness and the possibility of renewal in plays about royal families. Chap. 4 (113–222) begins with discussion of *Pericles*, stressing the importance of royal succession and genealogy. *Cym*, Bergeron believes, is similarly concerned with establishing national stability through succession, and the play resolves the conflict between political interests and personal desires in royal marriage. Bergeron criticizes Erickson's interpretation of patriarchal structure in *WT* (no. 158), arguing that establishing succession through Perdita emphasizes the importance of the female line. He also analyzes contrasting father/son relationships in the play. *Tmp* continues the themes of "peaceful succession" and "royal genealogy" (181), Bergeron believes, and adds a new concern with a union of kingdoms, parallel to the union of England and Scotland. This section stresses *Tmp*'s dramatization of epiphanies and of redemption in the fullness of time.

30. **Danby, John F.** "Sidney and the Late-Shakespearean Romance." In *Poets on Fortune's Hill*, 74–107. London: Faber and Faber, 1952.
Repr. Port Washington, N.Y.: Kennikat Press, 1966.

Danby interprets the romances in relation to the schematic moral universe of Sidney's *Arcadia*, stressing the virtue of patience in adversity. Although he praises Shakespeare's ability to provide "moral occasions" rather than "moral precepts" (96), Danby nonetheless argues that the romances lack the seriousness and verisimilitude of the tragedies.

31. **Dixon, Mimi Still.** "Tragicomic Recognitions: Medieval Miracles and Shakespearean Romance." In Maguire (no. 104), 56–79.

This essay establishes generic similarities between medieval miracle plays and Shakespeare's late plays. The tragicomic improbability of the miracle plays, Dixon emphasizes, leads us toward "a reflective self-consciousness about the limitations of human vision" (65); these plays also suggest that symbols "both express and obscure" (66) spiritual realities. Dixon argues that *Tmp*, *WT*, and *Cym* similarly juxtapose differing perspectives upon reality, reflecting upon the improbability of "the providential patterns of tragicomedy" (75). By questioning their own incredibility, she concludes, Shakespeare's last plays paradoxically provide "a critique of the notion of probability itself" (63); their vision of the miraculous is thus more enticing than that of many Renaissance plays whose tragicomic reversals have become a mere cliché.

32. **Dolan, Frances E.** *Dangerous Familiars: Representations of Domestic*

Crime in England, 1500–1700. Ithaca: Cornell Univ. Press, 1994.

This book's introduction (1–19) argues that literary representations of domestic violence in the early modern period seek to "restore the order threatened by ... insubordination" (13). The section on *Tmp* (chap. 2, 59–88, especially 59–71) discusses the relationship between Prospero and Caliban in terms of master-servant discourses. Dolan argues that the play represents rebellion as easily containable by relegating it to a comic, subordinate plot. Aesthetic order, she concludes, thus confirms social order. Chap. 4 (121–70) interprets *WT* in relation to treatments of infanticide and child abandonment in legal documents, popular pamphlets (including those that sympathize with murderous mothers as victims of poverty and abuse), and literary genres such as romance. Dolan maintains that "as the play moves out of tragedy and into romance, it displaces blame for [Leontes'] angry repudiation of the baby" onto subordinates who carry out his orders (166). For Dolan, *WT* prepares us to forgive Leontes by aestheticizing his attempt at child murder, associating it with the romantic fantasy of the return of a "lost" child and familial reconciliation. She concludes that *WT* exemplifies a process of canon formation in which politically orthodox works are those that survive. An earlier version of chap. 2 appeared as "The Subordinate('s) Plot: Petty Treason and the Forms of Domestic Rebellion," SQ 43 (1992): 317–40.

33. Gesner, Carol. *Shakespeare and the Greek Romance: A Study of Origins.* Lexington: Univ. Press of Kentucky, 1970.

This book traces (chaps. 1 and 2, 1–46) the influence of Greek romances on medieval and Renaissance European literature. Chap. 3 (47–79) discusses the influence of this tradition on *Comedy of Errors, Twelfth Night, Romeo and Juliet, Much Ado about Nothing, Othello*, and *As You Like It*. In chaps. 4 and 5 (80–143), Gesner argues that recognizing the extensive influence of the Greek romance and its descendants upon *Pericles, Cym, WT*, and *Tmp* helps to explain these plays' abandonment of literal realism and their movement "through travail and vicissitude toward a world of golden perfection" (82). She concludes that Shakespeare's multifaceted symbolism ennobles the improbable fictions of the romance genre.

34. Henke, Robert. *Pastoral Transformations: Italian Tragicomedy and Shakespeare's Late Plays.* Newark: Univ. of Delaware Press; London: Associated Univ. Presses, 1997.

This book examines *Cym, WT*, and *Tmp* as pastoral tragicomedies influenced by Italian theory and practice and by English social and theatrical contexts. Chap. 1 (13–44) establishes a methodology that includes both the study of influences and examination of parallel developments in England and Italy. In chap. 2 (45–65) Henke examines the influence of Italian pastoral tragicomedy and commedia dell'arte on English Renaissance plays, and in chap. 3 (66–77) he discusses Cinquecento theory concerning the emotional, cognitive, and ethical dimensions of theater. Chap. 4. (78–106) explores the relation between idealized "soft" pastoral and tragic themes in Tasso, Guarini, and Shakespeare. Henke also comments on the negotiation between verisimilitude and the marvelous, especially in *WT*. Chap. 5 (107–19) surveys classical and Renaissance treatments of satyrs as possible precedents of Caliban. In Chap. 6 (120–40), Henke argues that Shakespeare's late plays modulate audience responses through narrative and rhetorical devices that produce "diminished terror, pathos, and wonder" counterpointed by "popular farce" (134). Chap. 7 (141–53) argues that the mixture of generic signs in these plays produces shifting horizons of expectation in the audience. Henke maintains that changes of place are changes of culture, and characters' behavior is often more a function of the location of the action than a reflection of realistic psychology. Chap. 8 (154–65) discusses the dialogues among the points of view associated with tragic, comic, satiric, and pastoral modes in *Cym*, *WT*, *Tmp*, and Italian tragicomedy; in chap. 9 (166–81), Henke considers the social implications of generic and modal interaction, concluding that Shakespeare is more attracted to "social lability and interclass alliances" (175) than other dramatists. His primary example is *WT*'s integration of Bohemian pastoral characters, including the Shepherd and Clown, into the Sicilian court. Chap. 10 (182–98) treats the integration of low comedy, associated with the lower classes, into plays that combine a range of genres and theatrical styles.

35. James, Heather. *Shakespeare's Troy: Drama, Politics, and the Translation of Empire.* Cambridge: Cambridge Univ. Press, 1997.

This book analyzes Shakespeare's transformation of his sources in order to illuminate his ambivalent treatment of the ideology of empire. Chap. 5 (151–88) argues that *Cym* characterizes Posthumus as national hero in the tradition of Aeneas, while personal and national corruption appear in the form of the subtle Italian, Iachimo. Yet James believes that *Cym* reverses the Roman ethic that demands Aeneas's rejection of Dido and his devotion to a rigid, masculine, warrior's ethic in that Posthumus regains his virtue through love of Imogen and through questioning the misogynistic social code that contaminated his personality. In the denouement, James argues, Posthumus is displaced as potential heir to the throne by Cymbeline's sons, and this separation of familial from imperial integration contributes to *Cym*'s diffusion of authority and its interrogation of James I's absolutist rhetoric. Chap. 6 (189–221) discusses *Tmp*'s reflection of 17th-century challenges to the "paternalistic and hierarchical model of state and family" (192). James argues that

Tmp's transformation of the Aeneid (especially the play's focus on Dido) and its ambivalent treatment of Prospero's art suggest that Prospero cannot "coerce his subjects into compliance with Vergilian ideals" (210). *Tmp*'s epilogue, James concludes, reflects a constitutional model of government in which the monarch's power derives from consent of the governed. See also Tudeau-Clayton (no. 213).

36. Jordan, Constance. *Shakespeare's Monarchies: Ruler and Subject in the Romances*. Ithaca: Cornell Univ. Press, 1997.

This book argues that Shakespeare's romances dramatize the destructive consequences of tyranny and the providential process through which rulers who have abused power learn respect for law. Chap. 1 (1–33) discusses the tradition of constitutional monarchy that was challenged by Stuart absolutism; Shakespearean romance, Jordan suggests, demonstrates that "absolute rule ... easily degenerates into despotism, incites popular rebellion, and creates political chaos" (2). *Pericles*, Jordan believes (chap. 2, 35–67), focuses upon Antiochus's incest as an instance of tyrannical departure from natural law, and the story of Pericles' trials explores "the nature and scope of a ruler's art" (57) and its relation to divine powers. Chap. 3 (69–106) discusses *Cym* as founded on "contracts broken and then renewed" (100). Both Posthumus's relation to Imogen and Britain's relation to Rome are restored when characters regain their capacity to act in good faith; the image of the eagle vanishing in the western sun, Jordan believes, symbolizes the providential translation of empire from Rome to Britain, the latter superior to Rome because of its Christian foundation and its respect for the rights and consciences of the governed. Chap. 4 (107–46) argues that *WT* uses the analogy between the family and the state in order to affirm that royal authority must be tempered by a concern for equity that is founded on love. For Jordan, Leontes' megalomania leads him to act as though neither Polixenes nor Hermione can possess an independent will without committing treason; such tyranny is identified as impiety when Leontes ignores divine law. Paulina's art and the passage of time restore his capacity for love and faith and thus enable him to establish a "graceful monarchy" that respects "the place and office of each subject" (146). Chaps. 5 and 6 (147–209) describe Prospero's art as both royal power and theatrical illusion. At times, Jordan suggests, Prospero's use of his art to effect a return to Milan appears acceptable, but his abjuration of it may also imply that his occasional use of his power to deprive subjects of agency tends toward unacceptable absolutism. This section also discusses Prospero's achievement of the temperance and magnanimity necessary for fit rule, and it analyzes *Tmp*'s treatment of colonization in relation to Renaissance theories of just rule and tyranny.

37. **Pettet, E. C.** *Shakespeare and the Romance Tradition.* London: Staples Press, 1949. Repr. London: Methuen, 1970; and New York: Haskell House, 1976.

In chap. 1 (11–35) Pettet discusses the romance tradition, stressing the genre's idealization of love and its reliance on adventure, the marvelous, and extravagant plots. He attributes its pervasive influence on Renaissance literature to its appeal to aristocratic values and to the delight afforded (as Sidney and Spenser attest) by beauty and portrayals of good fortune. Chap. 7 (161–99) praises Shakespearean romance for its "vigour and excitement of narrative … unhampered by any considerations of verisimilitude" (163). Pettet argues that the last plays dramatize poetic justice tempered by mercy, but he believes that Tillyard (no. 84) places excessive emphasis on the theme of regeneration and on symbolism. Pettet emphasizes that the confrontation with evil in the romances distinguishes them from the romantic comedies, but he nonetheless regards Shakespeare's last plays as distanced from reality, especially by the lack of plausible motivation in the characters.

38. **Smith, Hallett.** *Shakespeare's Romances: A Study of Some Ways of the Imagination.* San Marino, Calif.: Huntington Library, 1972.

This book studies the workings of Shakespeare's imagination by comparing the romances with their sources and with earlier plays in Shakespeare's canon. Early chapters analyze the plays in the context of the prose romance tradition, emphasizing the lessons of patience amidst trials of fortune; discuss Shakespeare's innocent maidens in relation to their predecessors in pastoral literature; explore the evolution of Shakespeare's interest in wronged heroines and the quest for self-knowledge in the problem comedies and romances; and compare the treatments of patience and the journey through the "green world" in the romances and the tragedies. Smith's extensive comparison between Greene's *Pandosto* and *WT* emphasizes the naturalization of pastoral and the formalization of style; his study of *Tmp* in relation to *A Midsummer Night's Dream* discusses the relation between dreams and reality. Concluding sections discuss Shakespeare's methods of describing scenery and "landscape," which Smith defines as "that world which is described in visual terms but not shown visually on the stage" (145), and the complexity of his language and style. Throughout the study, Smith criticizes excessive emphasis on myth and religious symbolism, especially in appendix A (197–209). Appendix B (211–21) expresses skepticism concerning the topicality of *Cym* and *WT*.

39. **Tennenhouse, Leonard.** "Family Rites: City Comedy, Romance, and the Strategies of Patriarchalism." In *Power on Display: The Politics of Shakespeare's*

Genres, 147–86. New York: Methuen, 1986. Extract repr. in Ryan (no. 106b).

Tennenhouse sees all of Renaissance drama as sustaining monarchical and aristocratic power. He argues that the miraculous restorations of royal families in the romances assert a metaphysical foundation for genealogical patriarchy. For Tennenhouse, the errors of Cymbeline, Leontes, and Prospero represent threats to orthodox political ideology in that erring fathers act as though their authority were independent of the higher law that maintains continuity of the royal line; these threats are contained in *Cym*, *WT*, and *Tmp* as supernatural forces intervene to reinstate proper heirs to the throne and expand the power of the ruling family.

40. Thorndike, Ashley H. *The Influence of Beaumont and Fletcher upon Shakspere* [sic]. 1901. Repr. New York: Russell and Russell, 1965.

In chaps. 2–5 (9–96) Thorndike provides extensive discussion of the chronology, authorship, and stage history of Shakespeare's romances and the Beaumont and Fletcher canon, arriving at dates of 1609–10 for *Cym*, 1610–11 for *Tmp*, and 1611 for *WT*. This chronology leaves open the possibility that *WT* is later than *Tmp*. Having surveyed (chap. 6, 96–108) trends in genre development on the English stage from 1601–11, he concludes that the romances of Shakespeare and of Beaumont and Fletcher were a striking departure from dramatic tradition. Chap. 7 (109–32) credits Beaumont and Fletcher with originality in creating plots that are "equally ingenious and improbable, abounding in violent and unnatural situations" (110); notes that their characters are stereotypes; and comments on their innovations in poetic style and in the introduction of masques into plays for the public stage. Chap. 8 (133–51) discusses the following as evidence of Beaumont and Fletcher's influence on Shakespeare: the tragicomic form of the romances, especially the ingenious denouement; stereotyped characters; versification "aimed at producing an effect of natural and unpremeditated speech which should lend itself readily to action" (144); spectacular stage effects and masque-like elements. Chap. 9 (152–60) argues that Philaster (possibly written in 1608) probably influenced *Cym*, noting similarities in plot (including idyllic pastoral elements), characterization, and style. Chaps. 10 and 11 (161–69) argue that *WT* and *Tmp* transform elements of the Beaumont/Fletcher romances into plays more sophisticated and successful than *Cym*. See also Furness (no. 114), Nosworthy (no. 116), Wells and Taylor (no. 118), and Kirsch (no. 134).

41. Velz, John W. " 'Some Shall Be Pardon'd, and Some Punished': Medieval Dramatic Eschatology in Shakespeare." *Comparative Drama* 26 (1992–93): 312–29.

Velz discusses Shakespeare's creative use of eschatological motifs from medieval drama. He sees Leontes as a failed earthly judge who experiences penance and atonement. The play suggests dramatically, Velz believes, that "renewal is an inherently natural process" (323). *Tmp*, Velz argues, alludes to the emblematic Ship of Fools and to debates between Judgment and Mercy. Shakespeare's romances are comic, he concludes, because judgment is "corrective and tentative rather than punitive and definitive" (325), and the plays conclude with a new life in this world, rather than the end of history.

42. Yates, Frances. *Shakespeare's Last Plays: A New Approach.* London: Routledge and Kegan Paul, 1975. Repr. as *Majesty and Magic in Shakespeare's Last Plays.* Boulder, Colo.: Shambhala, 1978.

This book argues that Shakespeare's last plays participate in a Jacobean revival of hopes for universal religious and political reform that had been founded in part on occult philosophy and expressed in the Cult of Elizabeth. Yates believes that because James I offered little promise of universal reformation through a purified Protestant empire, revived hopes centered upon his children, Prince Henry and Princess Elizabeth. Chap. 2 (41–61) argues that *Cym* expresses hopes for universal peace under a reformed Christian empire established through the marriage of Elizabeth (Imogen) and Frederick, Elector Palatine (Posthumus). Chap. 4 (87–106) contends that *Pericles*, *WT*, and especially *Tmp* vindicate Renaissance magic as an instrument for moral and spiritual reform and express hope for regeneration effected by the younger generation.

See also nos. 49, 52, 58, 68, 75, 81, 106a.

B. Language and Linguistics.

43. Barton, Anne. "Leontes and the Spider: Language and the Speaker in Shakespeare's Last Plays." In *Shakespeare's Styles: Essays in Honour of Kenneth Muir*, ed. Philip Edwards et al., 131–50. Cambridge: Cambridge Univ. Press, 1980. Repr. in Ryan (no. 106b) and Bloom (no. 178) and in Barton, *Essays, Mainly Shakespearean*, 161–81. Cambridge: Cambridge Univ. Press, 1994.

Barton argues that in the last plays Shakespeare often creates an ironic discrepancy between the primary meaning of a speech and the speaker's understanding of his or her own words. This observation leads Barton to discussion of the questions these plays raise with regard to truth and falsehood, fiction and reality. She concludes that the romances lead us toward an awareness of our longing for an extraordinary reality expressed in fantastic tales.

44. Clemen, Wolfgang. *The Development of Shakespeare's Imagery.* 2nd edition. London: Methuen, 1977.

Clemen's purpose is to study the function of imagery in relation to "situation and character, plot and scenic action" (ix). Chap. 19 (182–94) argues that pervasive imagery of nature in *Tmp*—especially sea and storm, earth and vegetation—enables us to experience the island as a natural setting and, simultaneously, to sense that "this island is haunted" (191), that supernatural forces work through nature to influence human experience. Clemen also relates imagery to characterization, as when he notes that Caliban thinks in terms of concrete objects, rather than abstract concepts. Chap. 20 (195–204) analyzes images of disease and poison in relation to Leontes' passion and his eventual cure. Clemen also argues that imagery contributing to the atmosphere of idealized romance and the royal court (such as allusions to classical myth) is balanced by concrete reminders of the everyday world and country life, so as to suggest that renewal must be rooted in both realms. In chap. 21 (205–13), Clemen discusses the decorative imagery and formal rhetoric of *Cym*, relating it to characterization, as in the development of Belarius's reflective temperament, and the need to create a vivid natural setting for scenes involving the exiled warrior and his sons.

45. Hunt, Maurice. *Shakespeare's Romance of the Word.* Lewisburg, Pa.: Bucknell Univ. Press; London: Associated Univ. Presses, 1990.

Hunt discusses the destructive and redemptive powers of speech in the romances. *Pericles*, Hunt argues (18–40), dramatizes the redemptive power of bold speech that expresses ethical commitment and an active religious faith. The chapter on *Cym* (41–73) emphasizes the difficulty of expressing truth in imperfect human language: imperfect speech "creates the opportunity for the more conventional type of slander that pervades Cymbeline" (47), but ultimately those characters who respond appropriately to the experience of suffering learn the true meaning of words such as "faithful." Explication of the prophecy in act 5, Hunt concludes, demonstrates the reliability of divine speech as a guide for interpreting such experience. The chapter on *WT* (74–108) explores the ways in which situational contexts determine the significance of an utterance. Hunt suggests that Leontes misjudges Hermione's words by interpreting them in the "corrupt context" of "mad jealousy" (79), rather than the normal social context that promotes understanding. For Hunt, Paulina's speech becomes "the earthly vehicle of Apollo's providence" (88), and the play's final acts suggest that art provides a context for profound understanding and valuation of life. The chapter on *Tmp* (109–40) explores the manner in which corrupt, fallen language limits human self-knowledge and understanding of the world. Yet some characters—including Prospero himself—are led to redemption, Hunt argues, by reasoning that is stimulated by grace and enabled by rational speech. Hunt stresses the importance of visual symbols within such spectacles as the wedding masque (4.1), yet he also notes that visions must be interpreted by language. The conclusion (141–46) emphasizes that in Shakespearean romance idealized speech provides opportunities for redemption in a world often characterized by corrupt language.

46. Palfrey, Simon. *Late Shakespeare: A New World of Words.* Oxford: Clarendon Press, 1997.

This book argues that the rhetorical and linguistic practice of the late plays challenges patriarchy and political hierarchy and thus creates a "politically restless genre" (230). Palfrey notes, for example, that when Imogen embraces the dead Cloten her language is chaotic and vulgar; Caliban, in contrast, utters majestic poetry. He says that such breaches of decorum transgress conventional generic and political boundaries, creating a drama that explores new worlds of language and value. This study argues that through carnivalesque transformations of metaphors such as "the body politic" Shakespeare questions idealized conceptions of character and of social order; Palfrey also suggests that pastoral elements in the romances are potentially liberating, but too chaotic to promise sure regeneration. *Tmp*, he believes, carries furthest this tendency of "romance wilderness" to provide an imaginary realm of primordial origins "at once dystopian and utopian" (138) and characterized by "polyvalent creativity" (148).

47. Spurgeon, Caroline. "Leading Motives in the Romances." In *Shakespeare's Imagery and What It Tells Us*, 291–308. Cambridge: Cambridge Univ. Press, 1935. Repr. Boston: Beacon Press, 1958.

Spurgeon finds images of nature and rural life and of commerce the dominant strains in *Cym*. She discusses images of sound, especially of harmony and discord, in *Tmp*. Spurgeon argues that patterns of imagery in *WT* reflect Shakespeare's awareness of "the common flow of life through all things, in nature and man alike" (305).

48. Wright, George T. *Shakespeare's Metrical Art.* Berkeley and Los Angeles: Univ. of California Press, 1988.

Wright studies Shakespeare's verse in relation to the expression of nuanced and powerful thoughts and feelings appropriate to specific dramatic contexts. He places Shakespeare's verse in historical perspective and addresses the question of the relation between text and performance. Wright typically draws examples from a range of plays within each topical chapter. (Readers can find examples from specific plays by referring to his index.) He concentrates on the style of the romances (especially Prospero's final speech in *Tmp*) in 219–28.

See also nos. 38, 40, 49, 54, 55, 67, 71, 72, 74, 75, 81, 83, 84, 85, 92.

C. Criticism.

49. Adams, Robert M. *Shakespeare: The Four Romances.* New York: Norton, 1989.

Adams describes this introduction to the romances as an effort to illuminate Shakespeare's "translucent and delicate" texts with "a minimum of methodological apparatus" (xi, ix). Chap. 1 (3–23) discusses problems of genre and the relation between the romances and the preceding tragedies. Each of the following chapters discusses sources, plot structure, characterization, and poetic style in an individual play. Chap. 2 (24–57) also discusses the authorship of *Pericles*; emphasizes the play's theme of renewal; and argues that its characters are close to abstractions such as Innocence or Love. Chap. 3 (58–89) maintains that *Cym* is viable on the stage, despite its improbabilities, in part because of its patriotism and the appeal of Imogen. Adams discusses the relation between courtly and pastoral aspects of *Cym* and analyzes comparisons and contrasts among characters, especially Cloten and Posthumus. Chap. 4 (90–122) emphasizes *WT*'s methods of manipulating audience response, culminating in the final "coup de théâtre" (99) of the statue scene (5.3). Adams discusses *WT*'s classical allusions, mythic structure, and hints of visionary experience, and he interprets Autolycus as a joyful if mischievous storyteller, an embodiment of "capricious Shakespearean fancy" (102). In chap. 5 (123–57) Adams celebrates *Tmp*'s poetry and emphasizes the moods evoked by its imagery, and he criticizes symbolic, allegorical, and theological readings. Adams's conclusion (158–69) contrasts the straightforward "opaque carpentry" (165) of Beaumont and Fletcher with Shakespeare's suggestiveness—a "translucent" richness of implication that both entices and eludes an excessive "passion for subsurface exploration" (158).

50. Adelman, Janet. *Suffocating Mothers: Fantasies of Maternal Origin in Shakespeare's Plays, "Hamlet" to "The Tempest."* New York: Routledge, 1992. Extract on *Cym* from chap. 8 (200–219) repr. in Ryan (no. 106b).

This psychoanalytical study argues that rigid, aggressive masculine personalities in Shakespeare are formed in reaction against maternal origins perceived to be sources of contamination. Chap. 8 (193–238) interprets the romances as attempts to "reinstate the ideal parental couple lost at the beginning of Hamlet" (193); the plays record a struggle to escape the fantasy that links the evils of the fallen world to the sexualized maternal body. Adelman argues that Cymbeline's virtue and autonomy are restored by the death of the Queen, who is a symbolic "overwhelming mother" (202); the resolution centers upon a fantasy of an all-male family in which Imogen is displaced as heir to the throne by the king's restored sons. This ending, Adelman believes, concludes the play's dramatic constriction of Imogen's initially powerful selfhood. Adelman explains Leontes' jealousy in *WT* as fear of the maternal forces made visible in Hermione's pregnant body; *WT* grounds Leontes' recovery of masculine authority on his restored trust in Paulina and in the feminine realm of natural fecundity. This recuperation of the feminine is lost, Adelman concludes, in *Tmp*, in which Prospero's authority is founded upon banishment of the contaminated female body represented by Sycorax.

51. Barber, C. L., and Richard Wheeler. *The Whole Journey: Shakespeare's Power of Development.* Berkeley and Los Angeles: Univ. of California Press, 1986.

This book argues that Renaissance drama addresses psychological needs arising from family relationships. In chap. 1 (1–38), the authors assert that in Shakespeare's secular plays the reconciliations that prevent violence among fratricidal rivals are effected through human characters invested with a sacredness that enables them to displace the divine presences of the Catholic mass. Mature Shakespearean tragedy, Barber and Wheeler maintain, dramatizes the failure of the effort to develop a form of manhood in which compassion (associated with the maternal) "is as necessary as the ability to assert virile identity" (14). In *Pericles*, *Cym*, and *WT*, they believe, "Shakespeare recenters his art on the need men have to be validated by feminine presences, now dramatized as achieved in visionary reunions" (18). Chap. 10 (298–342) provides further commentary on the romances, primarily *Pericles*, *WT*, and *Tmp*. The authors emphasize that Leontes sees Polixenes as a father figure and rival for Hermione's love; reconciliation becomes possible vicariously through the union of Perdita and Florizel. In *Tmp*, they argue, the creative and restorative powers associated with the feminine are assimilated into Prospero's benevolent art, which enables the masculine ruler to transmit his authority to posterity without violence. *Tmp* also explores, they add, the power of theatrical art to change personalities. The passage of the young into adulthood through marriage, they conclude, enables the older generation to accept death. Portions of this study are based on Barber (no. 153).

52. Bieman, Elizabeth. *William Shakespeare: The Romances.* Twayne's English Authors Series 478. Boston: G. K. Hall, Twayne, 1990.

Bieman's introduction (1–18) discusses romance as a quest that results in transformation of the self. She relates this process to Christian theology and ritual, Neoplatonism and alchemy, and Jung's theory of psychic integration. Chap. 2 (19–41) provides a Jungian interpretation of Pericles as an idealistic "puer aeternus [perpetual youth]" who attains autonomy only when his quest for the perfect mother-wife-daughter is transformed into mature love of individuals. Chap. 3 (42–65) argues that *Cym* dramatizes the development of authentic love in both Imogen and Posthumus, thus revealing psychological complexity in both of them; the play's concluding scene, however, depicts Imogen as totally subjugated to her husband. Bieman also discusses the power of slander in *Cym* to undermine a social order built on trust. Chap. 4 (66–89) discusses Leontes' progress toward a capacity for love in terms of allusions to both Christianity and the pagan goddesses that preside over "great creating Nature." For Bieman, Florizel and Perdita both possess the balance of masculine and feminine qualities that characterizes a healthy personality. Chap. 5 (90–117) emphasizes the imagery of baptism and other Biblical allusions in *Tmp.* Central to the discussion is the transformation of Prospero himself, grounded on his acceptance of "the Caliban within" (113). Throughout this book, Bieman affirms the power of art to move us toward faith in the creative powers of life. Each chapter also includes a synopsis of the relevant play and discussions of date, text, and sources.

53. Bloom, Harold. *Shakespeare: The Invention of the Human.* New York: Penguin Putnam, Riverhead Books, 1998.

The preface and introduction to this book (xvii–xx and 1–17) claim not only that Shakespeare created realistic characters, but that he invented human personality as we now know it. For Bloom, Shakespeare has taught us to think and to perceive in ways previously unknown, and he has promoted an unprecedented degree of self-awareness; the playwright has thus expanded human consciousness. Chap. 31 (614–38) argues that much of the far-fetched plot, grotesque characterization, and inferior verse of *Cym* are Shakespearean self-parody. Bloom regards Imogen as the only character in the play who possesses the psychological depth and inwardness that is the hallmark of Shakespeare's greatness; placing her in *Cym* is a "juxtaposition of aesthetic dignity with the absurd" (618). Asserting that Shakespeare's plays are beyond generic definition, Bloom describes *WT* (chap. 32, 639–61) as a compound of "pastoral lyric," "psychological novel," and "grotesque comedy" (639, 660). He believes that Leontes' jealousy and misogyny are founded upon nihilism and paranoia; Leontes is a foil to the life-affirming rogue Autolycus and to Perdita, who "incarnates a heroic naturalism" (656). Bloom regards the statue scene (5.3) as puzzling rather than artistically successful. Chap. 33 (662–84) begins by dismissing virtually all political readings of *Tmp*: "Marxists, multiculturalists, feminists, nouveau historicists—the usual suspects—know their causes but not Shakespeare's plays" (662). Bloom regrets that Shakespeare lost interest in creating psychological inwardness in this "wildly experimental ... comedy" (663). He also laments Prospero's decision to resume political authority rather than pursue Hermetic magic; indeed, Bloom interprets Prospero's speech at 5.1.33–57 as more an assertion of power than a sincere recantation of art. Bloom is skeptical of readings that find unifying imagery or symbolism in the play. Although its purpose is to defend a tradition of criticism that reveres Shakespeare for his creation of personality and to critique more recent modes of interpretation, this book has no notes or bibliography.

54. Brown, John Russell. *Shakespeare and His Comedies.* 2nd edition, with a new chapter on the last comedies. 1962. Repr. London: Methuen, 1964.

Brown's chapter on the last comedies (205–52) argues that *Pericles*, *Cym*, *WT*, and *Tmp* dramatize a wider range of experiences than the earlier comedies, but they are nonetheless informed by similar ideals of friendship, love, and order. Analysis of contrasts, stage techniques, and imagery, Brown believes, can reveal the plays' implicit judgments upon human relationships. He focuses upon the works' subtle and intricate affirmations of the value of love, the truth perceived by characters whose imagination is informed by love, and the order established when genuine love informs social relations. He concludes that *Tmp*, despite its fantastic elements, ends more realistically than the other romances in its emphasis upon human imperfections.

55. Desmet, Christy. *Reading Shakespeare's Characters: Rhetoric, Ethics, and Identity.* Amherst: Univ. of Massachusetts Press, 1992.

Chap. 3 of this book (59–83) analyzes the uses of epideictic rhetoric (i.e., the rhetoric of praise and blame) to construct character in *Cym*. Arguing that the play's concern is with ethos, rather than psychology, Desmet discusses the play's contradictory constructions of the ethical characters of Imogen, Posthumus, and others, concluding that the play dramatizes both "the urge to evaluate ethical character and the difficulties attendant upon moral judgment" (63). Desmet maintains that *Cym* illuminates the ways that rhetoric provides constructions of ethical character that are in part fictional, yet nonetheless crucial to our efforts to "shape character by schooling the judgment" (82). (Portions of chap. 3 appear in revised form in Teague [no. 108].) Chap. 4 (84–111) explores the role of hyperbole in constructing identity and judging character in *Othello*, *King John*, and *WT*. Desmet examines how Leontes' "hyperbolic metaphors" (106), such as his reading of himself as "knowing cuckold" and therefore "poisoned man" (106–7), lead to the false conclusion that "All's true that's mistrusted" (2.1.48), thus overwhelming Hermione's valid self-defense. The chapter concludes with discussion of more appropriate uses of hyperbolic metaphor to convey the speaker's generous attitude in Florizel's description of Perdita (4.4.135–46) and Leontes' reading of Hermione's "statue" in 5.3. Desmet makes judicious use of rhetorical and literary theorists from Aristotle through Erasmus to Kenneth Burke and Paul de Man, and she provides numerous illuminating readings of Shakespeare's language and characterization.

56. Egan, Robert. *Drama Within Drama: Shakespeare's Sense of His Art in "King Lear," "The Winter's Tale," and "The Tempest."* New York: Columbia Univ. Press, 1975.

In chap. 1 (1–15), Egan argues that plays within the play in *King Lear*, *WT*, and *Tmp* explore the possibility that dramatic art may restore our faith in a natural order of love and thus enable us to reform fallen human society. Chap. 3 (56–89) discusses Camillo and Paulina as artists whose visions of love and order become reality. Camillo, Egan argues, creates a script to reconcile Florizel and Perdita to Leontes, and the apparent fiction becomes reality when Leontes embraces the young lovers and "the natural values they embody" (72). For Egan, Polixenes' assertion in act 4 that human art is a means through which nature improves itself is a key to the play's aesthetic. He concludes that the statue of Hermione (5.3) is presented as "a work of nature's art" (81), an image that reflects Leontes' unfallen reality, and, when the king exerts his faith in her, she comes to life. Chap. 4 (90–119) stresses that Prospero initially believes that his art can eradicate all traces of human evil; he fails to recognize that the audience must respond voluntarily to the vision if the artist is to succeed in his redemptive mission. The intrusion of reality into the idealized wedding masque (4.1) and Ariel's appeal to the magus to pity his enemies contribute to Prospero's self-knowledge and to his final vision of an art that can transform life through an acknowledgment of human evil and an act of faith informed by charity and forgiveness. The epilogue invites Shakespeare's audience to exert our faith in the artist's vision of love; if we have such faith, Egan concludes, our experience may be transformed by Shakespeare's art. This book includes a revised version of "'This

Rough Magic': Perspectives of Art and Morality in 'The Tempest,' *SQ* 23 (1972): 171–82.

57. Evans, Bertrand. *Shakespeare's Comedies.* Oxford: Clarendon Press, 1960.

Evans analyzes Shakespeare's use of discrepancies of awareness among characters and between characters and the audience. He argues that in earlier comedies the audience is assured of a comic resolution, but such assurance is denied in *Pericles, Cym,* and *WT.* He argues (245–89) that *Cym* is "Shakespeare's greatest achievement" (248) in the manipulation of discrepant awarenesses, generated primarily by the characters' deceptions of one another, for complex dramatic effect. The appearance of Jupiter in act 5, Evans concludes, prepares us for the reversal of fortunes and affirms the influence of a benign cosmic order. Evans argues (289–315) that *WT* goes further than *Cym* in seeming to deny the possibility of calm resolution of the "lasting storm" (289). Even the audience, he emphasizes, is denied knowledge of Hermione's survival until 5.2, when we are told of the statue and thus given a hint of the truth; this method provides both an element of surprise and a moment when we have an advantage of understanding over Leontes. The chapter on *Tmp* (316–37) emphasizes that Shakespeare provides assurance of a benevolent controlling power in 1.2, thus creating a consistently comic mood and a gap between our understanding and that of most of the characters. The presence of Prospero as a godlike power, Evans concludes, reduces dramatic conflict; the play's aesthetic interests are founded instead on poetry, music, spectacle, and the "satisfaction of seeing evil utterly helpless in the grasp of good" (337).

58. Felperin, Howard. *Shakespearean Romance.* Princeton: Princeton Univ. Press, 1972. Chap. 7 repr. in Hunt (no. 179). Excerpt from chap. 8 repr. in Bloom (no. 100).

In chap. 1 (3–54) Felperin defines romance as "a success story in which difficulties … are overcome … against impossible odds or by miraculous means" (10). Surveying the influences of ancient and medieval romance and medieval drama, Felperin argues that English Renaissance romances stressed the acquisition of virtue by trial. Shakespearean romance, he suggests, qualifies the virtues of its heroes and problematizes its triumphs, thus re-examining the conventions of the genre. Chap. 2 (57–70) argues that individual and social reformation is less difficult in the romantic comedies than in the last plays; the latter incorporate genuinely tragic elements, and their resolutions intensify our sense of the miraculous. In chap. 3 (71–96), Felperin maintains that *Troilus and Cressida, All's Well That Ends Well,* and *Measure for Measure* express an intensified ambivalence toward the romantic vision of life, and chap. 4 (97–139) argues that the major trage- dies typically raise "romantic expectations only to defeat them with tragic actualities" (117–18). In chap. 5 (143–76) Felperin emphasizes that *Pericles* utilizes the conventions of medieval religious drama to enable the audi- ence to accept the play as a parable of miraculous reformation. Chap. 6 (177–210) discusses the fusion of history and romance in *Cym* and *Henry VIII*, stressing the progression in these plays from the order of nature (characterized by legalism and vengeance) to the order of grace (character- ized by mercy and forgiveness). Felperin argues that these two plays are distanced from a modern audience through their efforts to promote "a mythic realm of a Tudor golden age" (208). *WT*, in contrast, Felperin argues (chap. 7, 211–45), creates an impressive fusion of realistic character- ization and romance structure. For Felperin, characters in *WT* are vivified by lifelike details, yet they simultaneously remind us of the personified vices and virtues of religious drama; the dialogue is both natural and oracular; and *WT*'s emphasis on rebirth is reinforced by parallels to the cycles of nature. This chapter concludes that *WT* celebrates the miracu- lous restorative art made possible through Camillo and Paulina even as it persuades us of the reality of human loss. Chap. 8 (246–83) discusses the dialectic between romantic and anti-romantic aspects of *Tmp*. Felperin argues that, even though Prospero renounces vengeance and strives to use benevolent art to reform individuals and restore social harmony, the play insistently reminds us that the magician's project cannot totally transform mundane reality into the golden world of romance. A "Bibliographical Appendix" (287–316) evaluates critical opinion on Shakespeare's romances from early responses through Dryden and Johnson to Knight and Frye.

59. Foakes, R. A. "Shakespeare's Last Plays." In *Shakespeare: The Dark Comedies to the Last Plays: From Satire to Celebration*, 94–172. London: Routledge and Kegan Paul; Charlottesville: Univ. of Virginia Press, 1971.

Foakes argues that in the last plays Shakespeare developed techniques for "distancing the action and characters, and disengaging our sympathies and moral commitment" (97) in order to focus on patterns of events that point toward a marvelous but inscrutable providence. *Cym* and *WT*, Foakes believes, portray characters as manipulated by providential forces that they do not comprehend, rather than by human agents whose actions determine the outcome of the plot. Foakes believes that Cymbeline's and Leontes' destructive anger and subsequent reformation must be under- stood in terms of capricious fortune and divine intervention rather than realistic psychology, and that characters such as Autolycus and Paulina, while they seem to control others, are themselves merely agents of larger, mysterious forces. *Tmp*, Foakes maintains, develops in a new direction by giving us "in Prospero a controller who exercises through his magic a power like that of heaven" (145). Although Prospero's art is limited, Foakes concludes, it provides a vision, especially in the wedding masque, of a cosmic order that sanctions the social order restored at the play's conclusion.

60. Frye, Northrop. *Anatomy of Criticism.* Princeton: Princeton Univ. Press, 1957.

This book develops in comprehensive form Frye's theory connecting literature to myths, rituals, and archetypes. *Cym*, *WT*, and *Tmp* are mentioned frequently in *Anatomy*'s theoretical discussions, especially the section on comedy as the mythos of spring and regeneration (163–86). Bohemia in *WT* and Prospero's island in *Tmp*, Frye believes, are examples of the "green world" or "golden world" that embodies our dream of an ideal existence. Characters' experience of the green world, Frye argues, may result in personal and social renewal. See also additional items by Frye (nos. 61, 62, 102).

61. Frye, Northrop. *A Natural Perspective: The Development of Shakespearean Comedy and Romance.* 1965. Repr., with foreword by Stanley Cavell, New York: Columbia Univ. Press, [1995]. Chap. 2 repr. in Bloom (no. 100).

In this general introduction to Shakespearean comedy and romance, Frye argues in chap. 1 (1–33) that the romances are the culmination of Shakespeare's interest in technical aspects of dramatic form. Unlike history or tragedy, Frye believes, the romance genre eschews literal verisimilitude in favor of stylized conventions and thematic repetitions that are reminiscent of musical—especially operatic—structure. Chap. 2 (34–72) develops Frye's suggestion that this structure is grounded in primitive myth and ritual. Frye's comments on *Cym* in this section emphasize the characters' blindness and the play's providential structure. This analysis suggests that the romances dramatize "not merely an order but a power, at once supernatural and connatural, expressed most eloquently in the dance and controlled either by benevolent human magic or by a divine will" (71). Chap. 3 (72–117) discusses the tripartite structure of Shakespearean comedy and romance. The first stage, according to Frye, is an "anticomic society" (73) characterized by the destructiveness of irrationally harsh law or "a jealous tyrant's suspiciousness" (as with Leontes in *WT*). The second stage, he maintains, entails carnivalesque license, confusion, and loss of identity; in the festive conclusion all or most of the characters find both their singular identity (through self-knowledge) and their

social identity. Frye observes that alienated characters (e.g., Shylock, Mal-
volio, Leontes, Caliban) provide contrasting perspectives on the idealized
world toward which the play moves; many, though not all, are integrated
into the renewed society of the festive conclusion. Chap. 4 (118–59) explores the relation between Christianity and Shakespeare's vision of a
miraculous "golden world" (142) of renewal. Frye notes the association of
Shakespeare's vision of a better world with education and the arts, especially in *WT* and *Tmp*. Cavell's 1995 foreword (ix–xx) praises Frye's combination of rhetorical wit and profound insight. Cavell suggests that Frye
raises questions (e.g., whether art can communicate across cultural boundaries) that are still unresolved. See also additional items by Frye (nos. 60,
62, 102).

62. Frye, Northrop. *Northrop Frye on Shakespeare.* Ed. Robert Sandler.
Markham, Ontario: Fitzhenry and Whiteside, 1986.

This book offers interpretive comments based on Frye's classroom
lectures. The chapter on *WT* (154–70) observes that the play is comprised
of two stories: (1) the Leontes-Hermione plot, emphasizing the redemptive power of grace; and (2) the Florizel-Perdita story of young love
triumphant over the opposition of the older generation. Both stories,
Frye suggests, operate on three levels: (1) the lower or demonic level of
brute natural force uncontrolled by human art or reason; (2) the level of
rationality and civilization; (3) the realm of creative imagination and
wonder, suggested by the restoration of Perdita and the apparently
miraculous rebirth of Hermione. The final chapter (171–86) stresses that
Tmp is about the production of a play by Prospero; all of the characters
(including Prospero himself) embark on a quest, undergo an ordeal, and
experience imaginative visions. Ultimately, Frye argues, the quality of
one's dreams is the test of one's character, and the most noble dream is a
utopian one in which "both nature and human society [are] restored to
their original form" (186). See also additional items by Frye (nos. 60, 61,
102).

63. Girard, René. *A Theater of Envy: William Shakespeare.* New York:
Oxford Univ. Press, 1991.

Girard argues that Shakespeare reveals the importance of "mimetic
desire" in human relations. Shakespearean characters who wish to be
envied, Girard believes, create (through praising an object of desire that
they possess) actual rivals or imaginary ones. Girard stresses that, as
mimetic desire intensifies, one seeks to destroy one's rival. Chaps. 33 and
34 (308–20) argue that in *Much Ado about Nothing* and *Othello* Don John
and Iago serve as scapegoats on whom the audience can blame their own

jealousies; Leontes in *WT* is a more
self-generated nature. Posthumus's co
suggests, foreshadows the more profoun
in *WT*. Chap. 35 (321–26) discusses Sh
through which men blame women for
33), Girard argues that Paulina's claim t
is a satirical critique of Renaissance arti
Chap. 37 (334–42) emphasizes that Leon
the vain attempt to expiate his sins by de
only when he is certain that he is forgiv
discusses Prospero as a "hypermimetic" ch
envy his dukedom. Girard argues that Sh
pero as a playwright who enjoys but ultir
vengeful control over his enemies.

64. Grene, David. *Reality and the Heroic*
Shakespeare, and Sophocles. Chicago: Univ. o

This book discusses three authors' effort:
the events of life, looking backward from
section on Shakespeare (37–109) focuses upo
dramatic worlds: a real world flawed by hun
imaginary realm in which evil can be reforn
argues, begin in a corrupt society and concluc
life. *Cym*, he believes, most resembles the fairy
"artificially triumphant" (67), while *WT* reflec
"real life transformed into a fairy tale or a fair
Tmp, he suggests, is an extended study of a real
strives to reform human existence, yet elements
the play proceeds. All three plays, Grene conc
intractability of evil, and yet they ask us whethe
visions of a better life may become reality.

65. Hartwig, Joan. *Shakespeare's Tragicomic Vision*
ana State Univ. Press, 1972.

In chap. 1 (3–33) Hartwig argues that in the
characters aspire toward some perfect relationship; t
and finally the original wish is fulfilled in a manr
characters amazed", (4–5). She demonstrates that the
theatricality helps to balance engagement and detachr
a tragicomic vision: these plays reveal the identity o
of tragic human error and the ostensibly fabulous rea

action ma
nates the
the mixt
reunion
three pl
involvin
Cymbeli
external
Posthun
broaden
comple
its tragi
4 (104–
"fixed
Discuss
stresses
to shar
(131)
under
enlarg
persp
denti
coop
of th
visio
ing t
spirit

66.
Kay

deve
beli
ity"
con
im
fat
rh

67
Pl
Pe

kes possible a comic reversal of fortune. Chap. 2 (34–60) illumi-
pattern of loss and restoration that unifies *Pericles*, emphasizing
ure of realism and wonder in the revival of Thaisa and the
of Pericles and Marina. In chap. 3 (61–103) Hartwig discusses the
ts of Cym: the Imogen-Posthumus romance, the history play
Britain and Rome, and the pastoral story of Belarius and
ne's lost sons. She analyzes various complex relations between
appearances and inner realities, stressing that characters such as
us and Imogen purify their inner selves through trials that
their vision. Hartwig argues that the characters of *Cym* are more
than those of melodrama and that the play as a whole maintains
comic tone through comic presentation of serious themes. Chap.
6) focuses upon various means through which *WT* dislocates our
perceptions" (117) and thus sustains a tragicomic perspective.
ing such devices as the use of Time as narrator in 4.1, Hartwig
that "moving in and out of [theatrical] illusion" (128) prepares us
e Leontes' wonder in the statue scene (5.3), an "actualized dream"
hat brings us to experience the limitations of a purely rational
tanding. In chap. 5 (137–74), Hartwig argues that Prospero's art
es the vision of other characters by dislocating their mundane
ctives; it thus enables the integration of human action and provi-
l design. Yet Prospero's magic works only for those who choose to
rate with it; the epilogue, she concludes, assigns to the imagination
e audience the power to recognize the reality of *Tmp*'s magical
n. The conclusion (175–79) re-emphasizes the importance of recogniz-
he wonderful within the commonplace as a step toward social and
ual harmony.

Hoy, Cyrus. "Fathers and Daughters in Shakespeare's Romances." In
and Jacobs (no. 102), 77–90.
Hoy discusses father-daughter relationships in the romances as a
lopment of similar relationships in the tragedies. The last plays, Hoy
eves, strive to purge the imagination of visions of "female monstros-
(81) embodied in such characters as Goneril and Regan and to
struct images of "female purity that will have the effect of saving the
gination from despair" (81). Shakespeare was moved so deeply by the
er-daughter relationship, Hoy believes, that the plays' "mysterious
rthms of suffering and grace" (77) are derived from it.

Hunt, Maurice. *Shakespeare's Labored Art: Stir, Work, and the Late
ys. Studies in Shakespeare*, ed. Robert F. Willson, Jr., 3. New York:
ter Lang, 1995. Chap. 5 repr. in Hunt (no. 179).

This book discusses the late plays in the context of early modern attitudes toward labor. In chap. 1 (1–26), Hunt argues that the middle-class, protestant affirmation of the dignity of labor failed to reform a society often characterized by aristocratic indolence and working-class poverty and unemployment. He also discusses childbirth as the principal labor of women and the literary metaphor of intellectual work as child-birth. In chap. 2 (27–69) Hunt argues that from *Hamlet* through *Timon of Athens* Shakespeare increasingly affirms redemptive labor, and in chap. 3 (71–94) he elucidates the emphasis on socially beneficial and redemptive work in Pericles, including Cerimon's art and Pericles' acts of charity. Chap. 4 (95–133) contrasts the Queen's perverse conception of work as Machiavellian policy, Cloten's vicious indolence, and the labor that results in "spiritual refinement" (114) for Imogen and Posthumus. Imo-gen's labor as Fidele and Posthumus's work as a soldier, Hunt believes, sanctify these characters who have been saved by grace. The style of *Cym*, he concludes, reflects a world in which "Communication and understand-ing are special labors in the world of a god who values painful striving" (125). In chap. 5 (135–62) Hunt contrasts the natural labor of childbirth with the perverse "issue" of Leontes' imagination. He then argues that Perdita's festive labor in 4.4 inspires Florizel's lyric (4.4.135–46), a work that "legitimizes [Perdita's] being" (149) and thus rectifies Leontes' decep-tive imagination (1.2.135–46). Hunt also contrasts Paulina's redemptive art with the deceptive art of Autolycus. Chap. 6 (163–97) argues that Prospero's greatest success in *Tmp* is reforming Ferdinand's attitude toward redemptive labor; in other respects, Prospero's magic is only partially successful. For Hunt, Ariel's speech at 5.1 is "inspirational, nonmagical art" that evokes "ennobling sentiments" (190) of forgiveness within Prospero; Ariel's art thus parallels that of *Tmp* as a whole. Hunt concludes (259–78) by arguing that Shakespeare conceived his own art as spiritually redemptive.

68. Hunter, Robert Grams. *Shakespeare and the Comedy of Forgiveness.* New York: Columbia Univ. Press, 1965. Chap. 8 repr. in Hunt (no. 179).

This book analyzes the structure of *Much Ado about Nothing, All's Well that Ends Well, Cym, WT, Measure for Measure,* and *Tmp* in terms of a pattern of sin, repentance, and forgiveness. Having discussed medieval religious drama as well as the romance tradition as contexts for these plays, Hunter argues that the audience must understand sympathetically the contrition of characters such as Posthumus, Leontes, and Alonso in order to accept the denouement that results from these characters' being forgiven. Chap. 7 (142–84) describes *Cym* as a romantic comedy in which love is tested; Posthumus proves worthy of forgiveness through sincere contrition, as well as by charitably refraining from killing Iachimo in combat. Hunter sees *Cym* as the most overtly Christian of the romances, and he emphasizes the role of charity in sustaining personal and social relationships, yet he also stresses that mortals in this play recognize only with difficulty the operations of providence in a dramatic world in which the innocent suffer. Chap. 8 (185–203) argues that the gradual revelation of Hermione's restoration in 5.3 provides a denouement in *WT* superior to that of *Cym*. Hunter analyzes the mixture of good and evil in Leontes and the social consequences of the monarch's sin; although Shakespeare emphasizes the sufferings caused by human evil, *WT* nonetheless provides "Shakespeare's ... most powerful evocation of the wonders of human forgiveness and divine providence" (185). Chap. 10 (227–41) analyzes plot structure and iconography in *Tmp*. This chapter stresses the ineradicability of human evil; the plots of Antonio and Sebastian and of Caliban, Trinculo, and Stephano are analogues to the original plot against Prospero. Hunter sees the revelation of Ferdinand and Miranda in 5.1 as the denouement, as Ferdinand is restored to his repentant father. Hunter's conclusion (242–45) discusses Prospero's epilogue as summation of Shakespeare's effort to teach self-knowledge, contrition, and forgiveness.

69. Kahn, Coppélia. "The Providential Tempest and the Shakespearean Family." In Schwartz and Kahn (no. 107), 217–43. Repr. in *Man's Estate: Masculinity Identity in Shakespeare*, 193–225. Berkeley and Los Angeles: Univ. of California Press, 1981.

Kahn argues that tempest and shipwreck in *Comedy of Errors, Twelfth Night, Pericles, WT*, and *Tmp* symbolize the traumatic separation from the oedipal family that precedes the formation of mature masculine identity. In the romances, she believes, reconciliation with a daughter, who serves as "double" for the father and recapitulates his familial experience, makes it possible for him to accept sexuality and mortality. Leontes, she concludes, completes this process and becomes "both, and equally, husband and father" (240); Prospero, in contrast, bases his identity "entirely on his role as father, and his family is never united or complete" (240).

70. Kermode, Frank. *William Shakespeare: The Final Plays.* Writers and Their Work, no. 155. London: Longmans, Green, 1963. Extract on *Tmp* repr. in Graff and Phelan (no. 271a).

This 60–page book provides an introduction to the romances and a survey of criticism through 1963. Kermode analyzes plot structure and poetry in *Pericles, Cym, WT*, and *Tmp*, emphasizing the plays' roots in the romance tradition and their emphasis on repentance and regeneration. Kermode argues that the plays allude to Christian doctrine, both through language and in the various ways that they use scenes of recognition to suggest that time and chance are servants of providence. He is skeptical, however, about allegorical interpretations.

71. Knight, G. Wilson. *The Crown of Life: Essays in Interpretation of Shakespeare's Final Plays.* London: Oxford Univ. Press, 1947. Repr., with corrections, London: Methuen, 1958. Repr. New York: Barnes and Noble, 1966. Excerpt repr. in Muir (no. 180).

This book reprints Knight's 1929 essay "Myth and Miracle" (9–31), which affirms that the last plays embody mystical intimations of the triumph of love and creativity over despair, cynicism, and mortality. Knight focuses upon two symbols: the tempest that embodies "the turbulence of temporal events reflecting and causing tempestuous passion in the heart" (18) and the harmonious music associated with eternity and transcendent love. (See also Knight, no. 72.) Chap. 3 (76–128) discusses characterization and imagery in *WT*, emphasizing the triumph of "great creating Nature" over the forces of destruction represented by Leontes' sinful jealousy. Chap. 4 (129–202) discusses *Cym* as an expression of a British nationalism that acknowledges the importance of Roman tutelage during the nation's youth. Emphasizing the anachronistic distinction between Roman and Italian values in the play, Knight relates Shakespeare's characters to British virtues and foreign vices. He also argues that Posthumus's dream-vision in 5.4 concentrates *Cym*'s central emphasis upon providence and is integral to this play, rather than an interpolation by another author. (Cf. Furness [no. 114], Maxwell [no. 115], Warren [no. 117], and Wells and Taylor [no. 118].) Chap. 5 (203–55) argues that the action of *Tmp* is an extended metaphor that embodies the meaning of images and motifs that appear throughout the canon. Knight emphasizes the themes of separation in a storm, spiritual insight gained through loss of worldly power, and miraculous reunion. Prospero is the artist who reflects Shakespeare's power to preserve "a certain centre of faith or love" (222) while confronting tragedy and evil. He is also, Knight believes, an enlightened monarch whose wisdom embodies the genius of Great Britain. Throughout this study (which includes chaps. on *Pericles* and *Henry VIII*), Knight stresses that Shakespeare's language embodies a sense of wonder, an awareness of "mighty powers, working through both the natural order and man's religious consciousness, that preserve, in spite of all appearance, the good" (128).

72. Knight, G. Wilson. *The Shakespearian Tempest.* 3rd edition. 1953. Repr., with corrections, London: Methuen, 1964.

Knight believes that Shakespeare's dramatic universe is unified by the opposition between tempests (associated with discords, conflict, tragic loss, and mortality) and music (suggesting "love, concord, peace" [17], and restoration). Tempests are associated, he notes, with wild beasts and passion; harmony and love are associated with jewels and flowers. Chap. 5 (218–66) discusses the pervasive use of this symbolism in *Pericles, WT, Cym, Henry VIII*, and *Tmp*. Knight affirms that in these plays "there is ever a sense of personal divine powers controlling tempests" (227) and of mysterious justice in tragic experience. *Tmp*, he argues, "distils the poetic essence of the whole Shakespearian universe" (247) in its concentrated use of symbols used more fleetingly in other plays. For commentary, see Fox-Good (no. 226).

73. Lamb, Mary Ellen. "Engendering the Narrative Act: Old Wives' Tales in *The Winter's Tale, Macbeth*, and *The Tempest*." *Criticism* 40 (1998): 529–53.

This article uses social history and psychoanalytical theory to establish a distinction between tales told by women to children and the allegedly more serious literature mastered by males as a rite of passage into manhood. Lamb argues that *WT* 2.1 illustrates the "affective bond" (532) established through such tales; their sense of wonder also appears in Autolycus's storytelling. Lamb concludes that the play affirms Paulina's redemptive and feminine art. In *Tmp*, she argues, the distinction between Prospero's masculine, intellectual magic and the feminine, material witchcraft of Sycorax collapses, especially in 5.1, when Prospero's art is associated with Medea's witchcraft. Prospero's acceptance of maternal power may be a corollary of his acceptance of mortality, understood as a return to the "sea womb" (548) in which he drowns his book.

74. Derick R. C. Marsh. *The Recurring Miracle: A Study of "Cymbeline" and the Last Plays.* Lincoln: Univ. of Nebraska Press, 1962.

This book argues that the apparent improbabilities of the romances are subsumed into a pattern in which the attainment of virtues such as "piety, love and self-knowledge" (12) leads to reconciliation and to an affirmation of the "perpetual, miraculous renewal of life itself" (7) despite its tragedies and confusions. After a brief chapter on *Pericles* (13–24), Marsh provides scene-by-scene analysis of *Cym* (24–124), arguing that the play is unified around a set of related themes and around Imogen, who virtuously challenges the corruptions that affect most other characters. Marsh's close reading of the play's poetry and structure emphasizes images related to natural order; contrasts among characters, as when Imogen's altruistic love is juxtaposed to the possessiveness of Cymbeline and Posthumus and the total self-absorption of Iachimo; the idea that

"love consists in putting an unreasonable and individual value" (34) on
the loved person; the importance of sustaining one's faith in the value of
life despite one's misfortunes; and the relation between the acceptance of
mortality and a balanced evaluation of the self. Chap. 4 (125–61) traces
the development of these themes in *WT*. Marsh stresses that the play's
tragic events are the consequence of Leontes' and Polixenes' egocentricity;
the final reconciliations are made possible by their becoming "liberated ...
from the concerns of self" (156). Chap. 5 (162–91) explores the complexities
of *Tmp*'s characterization, structure, and attitude toward Prospero's art.
Marsh argues that the play dramatizes the spiritual transformations that occur
when characters commit themselves to love and when they learn to fulfill
and to control both their physical and their spiritual natures. The conclusion
(192–97) underscores Marsh's belief that Shakespeare's affirmation of the
value of life is founded upon faith in the natural, rather than the supernatural, order.

75. Marshall, Cynthia. *Last Things and Last Plays: Shakespearean Eschatology.*
Foreword by Arthur F. Kinney. Carbondale: Southern Illinois Univ. Press,
1991.
    Marshall interprets the romances in the context of the pervasive concern
with eschatology in the English Renaissance. Chap. 1 (1–11) introduces this
book's concern with "death, formal recapitulation, and thematic summation"
(2) in the last plays. In chap. 2 (12–37) Marshall discusses allusions to Advent
and Apocalypse in *Cym*. She stresses Cym's emphasis on physical mortality
as a reminder of impending judgment and the play's subsequent dramatization of a "collective deliverance" (36) that resembles Judgment Day: *Cym*'s
conclusion establishes a community based on the New Dispensation of
forgiveness. Chap. 3 (38–60) discusses Hermione's apparent resurrection and
her reunion with loved ones in *WT* (5.3) as "a proleptic vision of heaven"
(38). Marshall argues that the physicality of the reunion counters the mind-
body dualism of much Renaissance thought. For Marshall, Shakespeare's
dramatic fantasy of the restoration of family relationships offers a theatrical
wish fulfillment that was not provided by the orthodox Christian concept of
an afterlife in which there is no marriage. Chap. 4 (61–85) argues that the
narrative method of *Pericles* enables the audience "to view the events as might
God or an author or Gower himself" (62), drawing upon the typological
structure of the medieval mystery cycles. Yet in all of the romances, Marshall
believes, Shakespeare dramatizes a complex interaction between human
agency and divine providence. In chap. 5 (86–106) Marshall interprets Prospero's island and his art as expressions of the desire to escape the temporal
world and dwell in a transcendent paradise in which the wrongs of the past
will be rectified. Prospero's final abjuration of his art, she concludes, makes

possible his forgiveness of those characters whose mortality he finally acknowledges as his own. In chap. 6 (107–15) Marshall argues that "*The Tempest* flaunts drama's ability to take up and then discard various available paradigms for an ideal world" (114), and she suggests that fiction can stimulate "liberating directions for belief" (115) at times when the literal status of eschatological doctrine is questioned. Appendix A (119–21) compares theophanies in *Cym* and medieval Doomsday plays; appendix B (122–29) discusses the influence of resurrection plays on *WT*.

76. Mowat, Barbara. *The Dramaturgy of Shakespeare's Romances.* Athens: Univ. of Georgia Press, 1976.

Mowat describes Shakespearean romance as "open form" drama that eschews conventional forms of progressive unity and closure. She explores the manner in which *Cym*, *WT*, and *Tmp* provide a blend of comedy and tragedy, naturalness and artifice, engagement and detachment. The study emphasizes, for example, the intermingling of representational style (i.e., that which maintains an illusion of reality) and presentational style (that which calls attention to theatrical artifice and the fictive nature of the play). Structural devices, Mowat argues, especially a blend of narrative and dramatic modes, foil our expectations and evoke wonder and surprise, and this disruption of aesthetic coherence leads the audience to experience bewilderment. Thus, the author concludes, while Shakespeare's romances celebrate human "tenacity, faith and patience" (118), they also question the extent to which human reason can influence destiny or comprehend the mysterious forces that control human experience.

77. Nevo, Ruth. *Shakespeare's Other Language.* New York: Methuen, 1987. Chap. 5 repr. in White (no. 277a).

Nevo utilizes "post-psychoanalytical semiotics" to explore the relation between "unconscious signification, ... the language of dream and fantasy" and "rifts at the realist-rational level of plot, character and diction" (8). She seeks "an informing or generating fantasy, or ensemble of fantasies, in each play" (29), arguing that modern psychological interpretation can reveal the contemporary relevance of Shakespeare's romances. Chap. 2 (33–61) discusses *Pericles* in terms of the quest for full maturation of the psyche through liberation from sexual guilt and fear of incest. Chap. 3 (62–94) argues that the fantasy of regeneration in *Cym* centers upon the daughter who can bring new life; Shakespeare's romances thus add a fourth figure to the Freudian triad of "mother, wife and burying earth" (93). Chap. 4 (95–129) explains Leontes' jealousy as based upon fear of abandonment prompted by Hermione's bond with her unborn child; the reunions at the play's conclusion respond to the primal need for "transcendence of both isolation and of fusion, a harmony of needs, mutual recognition, freely expressed desire" (120). In chap. 5 (130–52) Nevo analyzes *Tmp* as a wish-fulfillment fantasy focused upon "happiness snatched out of disaster" (132). She discusses Shakespeare's influence on Freud's and Jung's analyses of the psyche, seeing Ariel as the urge toward sublimation and Caliban as the movement toward regression. For Nevo, Prospero achieves a psychic reformation that includes an element of mourning for human mortality.

78. Nosworthy, J. M. "Music and Its Function in the Romances of Shakespeare." *Shakespeare Survey* 11 (1958): 60–69.

Nosworthy demonstrates that music is used more extensively in the romances than in earlier plays, and he argues that music is "a regenerative, unifying and perfecting force" (66). In *Pericles* and *Cym*, Nosworthy believes, music signals contact between gods and mortals; music is prominent in the regenerative second half of *WT*; and it is pervasive in *Tmp*, the play that is the culmination of Shakespeare's development of an art in which "love [shapes] a new world out of chaos to the sound of music and the motions of the dance" (68).

79. Novy, Marianne. *Love's Argument: Gender Relations in Shakespeare.* Chapel Hill: Univ. of North Carolina Press, 1984.

This book focuses upon Shakespeare's treatment of conflicts between (1) mutuality and patriarchy and (2) emotion and control. Chap. 9 (164–87) argues that the romances emphasize the inadequacies of a conception of masculinity that valorizes Stoic self-control and denigrates affection and sensitivity. For Novy, Posthumus's and Leontes' misjudgments of women are clearly condemned, and female characters such as Paulina achieve a significant measure of independence; nurturing within families in the romances is highly valued; and military achievement is less important than familial reconciliation through forgiveness.

80. Peterson, Douglas L. *Time, Tide, and Tempest: A Study of Shakespeare's Romances.* San Marino, Calif.: Huntington Library, 1973.

Peterson interprets Shakespeare's romances as affirmations of faith in a morally coherent universe: *Cym*, *WT*, and *Tmp* are emblematic narratives that suggest the order behind appearances in the phenomenal world. The author suggests that Shakespeare draws upon the traditional image of life as a sea voyage and presents the tempest as a symbol of a trial that provides an opportunity for self-knowledge and reformation. Time in these plays, Peterson emphasizes, is cyclical; love is the force that renews human life in the world of mutability, and those characters with sufficient faith in providence and in their fellow human beings are granted opportunities to rectify errors of the past. This study illuminates the differences between the emblematic aesthetic of the romances and the representational mode of the histories and tragedies.

81. Platt, Peter G. *Reason Diminished: Shakespeare and the Marvelous.* Lincoln: Univ. of Nebraska Press, 1997.

Platt discusses the significance of wonder in the aesthetics of Shakespearean romance. Early chapters distinguish between an Aristotelian concept of wonder as merely the stimulus to rational inquiry and an alternative concept emphasized by Patrizi, Montaigne, and Shakespeare in which wonder destabilizes epistemological certainties and leads to intensified awareness of the limits of human knowledge. Platt treats these concepts in the context of Renaissance debates over religious imagery and ceremony, magic and science, and the ethical and social functions of literature. Arguing that wonder is a fundamental characteristic of aesthetic experience, Platt draws upon Mowat's view (no. 76) of Shakespearean romance as "open form" drama that eschews conventional forms of unity and closure and thus fosters ongoing inquiry. In *Cym*, for example, Posthumus is initially reduced to dogmatic nihilism by his misjudgment of appearances, yet he is eventually led, through the experience of wonder, to acknowledge his own ignorance. Similarly, Platt argues, *WT* presents Leontes' misjudgment of Hermione as the consequence of excessive faith in one's own reason and of the need for certainty. The play affirms the marvelous—including the wonder produced by theatrical artifice—as an antidote to the tyranny of the rational. Later chapters note that Shakespeare increasingly calls attention to his own art, yet he also raises questions concerning its power. For Platt, *Tmp* suggests that art can be seductive and lead us away from reality (as Prospero was led to abandon his political responsibilities in Milan), and yet it can provide a healthy skepticism concerning the human capacity to attain ultimate truth.

82. Rabkin, Norman. *Shakespeare and the Common Understanding.* New York: Free Press, 1967. Repr. Chicago: Univ. of Chicago Press, 1984.

Rabkin argues that Shakespearean plays are founded upon "complementarity," a vision of the paradox and "unresolvable complexity of life as life presents itself to the fullest human consciousness" (26). His chapter on the romances (192–237) stresses the plays' self-conscious theatricality and their paradoxical response to the powers of art and the imagination.

Cym, Rabkin emphasizes, averts tragedy by "the most implausible theatrical expedients" (207), and aspects of *WT*, such as the statue scene (5.3),
challenge credibility; yet both plays suggest that fantastic art may reflect
actual life, in which the miraculous restoration of grace and innocence
can occur. Rabkin traces numerous ways in which *Tmp* develops with the
greatest subtlety a comparison between theatrical art and human life,
suggesting, for example, that both can be beautiful if ephemeral, and both
may affirm the miraculous transformative power of love and forgiveness.

83. Stauffer, Donald A. *Shakespeare's World of Images: The Development
of His Moral Ideas.* New York: W. W. Norton, 1949. Repr. Bloomington:
Indiana Univ. Press, 1966. Excerpt repr. in Muir (no. 180).

Stauffer's chapter on the romances (266–311) discusses Shakespeare's
affirmation of patience, faith, repentance, integrity, love, and hope that
are miraculously rewarded after severe trial. Stauffer's discussion of *Cym*
emphasizes the importance of trust and the reality of goodness in spite of
the deceptive appearances that may cloak evil. He argues that Imogen is
a realistic portrayal of a virtuous woman, not an idealized symbol of
perfect virtue. Stauffer emphasizes the structural contrasts in *WT* between
jealousy and "purity, loyalty, and integrity" (293). Images of pastoral
innocence, he notes, precede final restoration of love and joy, and natural
beauty may reveal divine grace. Humor in *WT*, he suggests, complicates
moral judgments and hints at the contingency of the play's hopeful
vision. Stauffer regards *Tmp* as the final masterpiece in which moral ideas
are given "a dramatic body, or a musical structure, through repetitions
and variations and progressions" (302). Stauffer emphasizes the parallel
between Prospero and Shakespeare as artists whose imagination creates
characters and scenes that embody the essence of fear, joy, or wonder. He
compares the human artist to God, whose creation is "a visible symbol of
intelligence" (311).

84. Tillyard, E.M.W. *Shakespeare's Last Plays.* [1938.] Repr. New York:
Barnes and Noble, [1964]. Excerpt repr. in Muir (no. 180) and Langbaum
(no. 183).

Tillyard argues (16–58) that Shakespeare's romances extend the emphasis on regeneration that is adumbrated in the conclusions of the tragedies. Cymbeline, he suggests, errs in his banishment of Belarius and his
marriage to an evil queen; suffers retribution; repents; and is rewarded
with renewed prosperity. Plot and characterization in *Cym*, Tillyard adds,
attempt unsuccessfully to integrate elements of realism with the symbolism that Shakespeare adapted from Elizabethan prose romances. *WT*, he

believes, dramatizes the tragic pattern successfully: the first three acts realistically enact tragic destruction, and the final two provide the renewal embodied in Perdita, "at once a symbol and a human being" (44). Tillyard argues that *Tmp* achieves unity and concentration by subordinating the destructive phase and by making Prospero "the agent of his own regeneration" (50) and teacher of other characters. Tillyard also discusses (59–85) the combination of realistic and romantic elements in plot; realism and symbolism in characterization; and tragic style and "unearthly music" (74) in the plays' poetry. He concludes that this mixture of styles stimulates contemplation concerning the mysterious relations among different planes of reality in human experience. For commentary, see Pierce (no. 238a).

85. Traversi, Derek. *Shakespeare: The Last Phase.* London: Hollis and Carter, 1954; New York: Harcourt, Brace, and Co., 1955. Repr. Stanford: Stanford Univ. Press, 1965. Excerpt repr. in Muir (no. 180).

Traversi discusses the symbolic pattern of the last plays in which a family is divided through irrational passion; tragic suffering, often symbolized by the tempest, follows this division; and harmony is restored through repentance and mutual forgiveness. The book explores the manner in which poetic imagery and plot structure suggest a bond between individual experience and cosmic order. Traversi treats *Cym* as an early experiment that bridges, with only partial success, the realistic and symbolic modes. He discusses *WT*, whose form he compares to that of a symphony or ballet of four movements, as a more successful dramatization of the passage from innocence through conflict and discord to mature love, reconciliation, and fulfillment. He interprets *Tmp* as concentrating upon the final stage of this passage, in which providence provides characters the opportunity to develop mature wisdom. Traversi sees this emphasis on attaining regeneration through reflection upon tragic experience as the culmination of Shakespeare's development as a dramatist. A distillation of this book appears in *Modern Shakespearean Criticism*, ed. Alvin Kernan (New York: Harcourt, Brace and World, 1970), 427–47; and in *The Age of Shakespeare*, ed. Boris Ford, rev. edition, vol. 2 of *The New Pelican Guide to English Literature* (Harmondsworth, England: Penguin, 1982), 357–83.

86. Uphaus, Robert W. *Beyond Tragedy: Structure and Experience in Shakespeare's Romances.* Lexington: Univ. Press of Kentucky, 1981.

This book argues that Shakespeare's romances affirm regeneration and the "continuation of the life cycle generally" (3), thus going beyond the tragic focus on the value and the limitations of the individual. For Uphaus, tragedy ends with death as the "absolute close" (5) of life; in romance, death (literal or figurative) is subsumed in a larger providential order. After a section (12–33) on intimations of romance in *Macbeth, King Lear*, and *Antony and Cleopatra*, Uphaus discusses *Pericles* as "skeletal romance" in which the conventions of the genre are "displayed though rarely individuated" (34). The chapter on *Cym* (49–68) argues that the play's exaggerations render it a "genial parody" (53) of romance, and this explains why many of the play's outrageous events evoke laughter in the theater. Uphaus concludes that the play's excessive complications and its repeated emphasis upon mortal error produce an ending in which characters claim "a comprehensive awareness which is nowhere apparent" (68). Chap. 5 (69–91) discusses *WT* in terms of a tripartite structure in which sections of the play correspond to tragedy (acts 1–3), pastoral comedy (act 4), and romance (act 5). For Uphaus, the play's emphasis on the theme of "issue" is one way that it dramatizes the regenerative power of "great creating nature"; moreover, natural and human actions are transformed into "emblems ... of sacred experience" (87), as the play concludes with an affirmation of faith and wonder. Chap. 6 (92–117) maintains that Prospero's art creates experiences that characters interpret either in accordance with a belief in the possibility of regeneration or in ways that lead them merely to repeat the tragedies of the past. The apparent dissolution of art in acts 4 and 5, Uphaus concludes, is not a rejection of romance, but rather an affirmation that the artist's vision of mercy and forgiveness can become a reality in the actual lives of the audience. Chap. 7 (118–39) argues that *Henry VIII* dramatizes a providential view of history that develops further this tendency toward "the historical verification of the literary experience of romance" (122).

87. Wheeler, Richard P. " 'Since First We Were Dissevered': Trust and Autonomy in Shakespearean Tragedy and Romance." Schwartz and Kahn (no. 107), 150–69. Adapted from Wheeler's *Shakespeare's Development and the Problem Comedies: Turn and Counter-Turn*, 200–221. Berkeley and Los Angeles: Univ. of California Press, 1981.

Wheeler describes the development of Shakespeare's canon in terms of conflicting needs for "trust inseparable from the fear of destructive merger and [for] autonomy entangled with the threat of isolation and emptiness" (156–57). The romances move toward the establishment of a healthy identity in which the need for autonomy is balanced with "familial unity" (157). Wheeler argues that Leontes experiences a fantasy of omnipotence rendered destructive by a need for absolute power; he finds constructive identity when reunited in mutuality with Hermione, the maternal presence who survives the destructive phase of the action. In *Tmp*, Wheeler believes, maternal nurture is incorporated into Prospero's magic; "the need for autonomy is purged of the drive toward omnipotence" when Prospero accepts his "human limitations" (165).

88. Williamson, Marilyn L. *The Patriarchy of Shakespeare's Comedies.* Detroit: Wayne State Univ. Press, 1986.

In her introduction (11–24) Williamson advocates an alliance between feminism and the analysis of power relations developed by new historicism and cultural materialism. Chap. 3 (111–75) argues that *Tmp* demystifies the myth affirmed in *Pericles, Cym,* and *WT* that patriarchal authority is grounded in a benevolent natural order. For Williamson, rulers in *Cym* and *WT* at first appear tyrannical but are subsequently reformed, and the plays thus dramatize the continuation of a male dynasty ordained by providence. She argues that in *Pericles, Cym,* and *WT* contradictions make patriarchal structures "seem invulnerable to difference" (138), whereas *Tmp*, in contrast, reveals that providence is a product of the human imagination, thus subverting the myth affirmed in previous romances. Prospero's confession of the limitations of his art, she concludes, disrupts the parallel between fictional magic and absolutist political power.

89. Young, David. *The Heart's Forest: A Study of Shakespeare's Pastoral Plays.* New Haven: Yale Univ. Press, 1972.

Young discusses *As You Like It, King Lear, WT,* and *Tmp* in relation to the pastoral mode. Chap. 4 (104–45) argues that the romances explore the character and value of art and the human imagination; the pastoral elements in *Cym* and *WT* intensify the plays' questions concerning art and nature. Young's formalist analysis of *WT* stresses the role of Time as shaper of the story; the contrast between linear time and cyclical, restorative time; and the relativity of such contraries as tragedy and comedy. Chap. 5 (146–91) argues that the self-conscious theatricality of *Tmp* and its emphasis on magic and dreams produce a "sense of the basically illusory character of experience and of firm categories" (178). Young discusses *Tmp*'s revelation of the power of art to represent nature, to project ideals, and to stimulate self-knowledge. An appendix (196–204) advocates a mixture of stylization and realism in performances of Shakespeare's pastoral plays.

D. Stage History; Performance Criticism;
Film and Television Versions.

90. Brockbank, Philip, ed. *Players of Shakespeare: Essays in Performance by Twelve Players with the Royal Shakespeare Company.* Cambridge: Cambridge Univ. Press, 1985.

Following Brockbank's introduction (1–10) on the actor's craft in relation to text, director, and audience, this collection provides twelve actors' accounts of how they have created Shakespearean characters. Three essays deal with *Cym, WT,* and *Tmp.* Roger Rees (139–52) emphasizes Cym's ironic, sometimes humorous, perspective on Posthumus's foolishness. Gemma Jones (153–65) discusses the challenge of making Hermione's purity dramatically interesting. David Suchet (167–79) stresses Caliban's humanity and his character as "quintessential native" (179) who believes in black magic. While these actors acknowledge the validity of a range of interpretations, all emphasize the importance of sustained concentration on the evidence of the text.

91. Goldman, Michael. "The *Winter's Tale* and *The Tempest.*" Chap. 9 of *Shakespeare and the Energies of Drama,* 124–50. Princeton: Princeton Univ. Press, 1972.

Goldman discusses the theatrical experiences in *WT* and *Tmp* that afford us a vision of a restorative natural order that encompasses and transforms the tragedy of individual mortal lives. He argues that the "gestures of sympathy and generosity" that the romances provide are "emblems which suggest that a conformity exists between natural processes and our deepest intuitions of human kindness" (126). Goldman explores *WT*'s variations, culminating in the statue scene (5.3), on the suggestion that art evokes wonder because it embodies a truth about "great creating nature." The director of *Tmp,* he argues, must cultivate the sense of strangeness that reminds us of "the power of kindness in life" (149).

92. Warren, Roger. *Staging Shakespeare's Late Plays.* Oxford: Clarendon Press, 1990.

Although Warren provides comparative discussion of numerous performances, this study is based primarily upon his experiences in attending rehearsals and performances of the National Theatre's productions of *Cym, WT,* and *Tmp,* directed by Peter Hall, in 1987–88, and (secondarily) of *Pericles* (directed by Richard Ouzounian) and *WT* (directed by David William) at the Shakespeare Festival in Stratford, Ontario, in 1986. Warren emphasizes the advantages of Hall's involving "everyone—cast, stage management, observers—in a very open discussion of the play" (4) and of his beginning with close examination of the text rather than a preconceived concept. Warren argues that the "theatrical virtuosity" of the late plays serves not to distance the audience, but rather to startle us into focusing "maximum attention upon the ... emotions and situations that are displayed on the stage in an extreme form—love, despair, jealousy, death and burial, reconciliation and forgiveness—and it is this theatrical focus on emotional extremes which makes the plays so exhilarating" (6). Warren also argues that performances are enriched by the dramatization of the late plays as spiritual, purgatorial journeys in which "the extremes of love and joy [are] powerfully set against those of cruelty and loss" (243). He describes in detail the evolution of the costuming, set design, and interpretations of the structure, characters, action, and especially the language of each play. Warren provides many analyses of language in relation to character, as when Hall discussed "Innogen's habit of verbalizing her emotions, using often minute verbal details to pin down precisely what she thinks and feels" (29). Commentary on *WT* includes analysis of the manner in which Leontes' lines reveal a combination of paranoia and a subconscious desire for spiritual renewal (e.g., 1.2.237–41). Warren also argues that the creation of Paulina as Leontes' complex antagonist and spiritual guide is "one of Shakespeare's most remarkable and original achievements" (113). Discussion of Hall's *Tmp* production highlights the surrealistic visual and auditory effects that suggest, rather than attempt to portray literally, such events as the opening storm, a mirror of the internal storm that is Prospero's "purgatorial experience" (162). Warren concurs with Hall's opinion that the harmonious resolution of *Cym* is all-inclusive; that of *WT* is "muted" (93); and the ending of *Tmp* is by far the most incomplete, with the epilogue an appropriate recognition of Prospero's own need to be forgiven. The volume includes 15 photographs of performances and 11 rehearsal sketches by Alison Chitty. Combining Warren's and Hall's insights with those of other theater professionals, this book provides illuminating commentary on the plays. (Act, scene, and line numbers and the spelling of characters' names in this annotation are from the Compact Edition of the Oxford Shakespeare [see no. 3]; Hall and Warren both find the innovations of this edition significant for interpretation.)

See also nos. 48, 49, 89, 94, 95, 97, 105.

E. Reception History; the Late Plays as Source for and Influence on Later Writers and Works.

93. Cohn, Ruby. *Modern Shakespeare Offshoots.* Princeton: Princeton Univ. Press, 1976.

Cohn's chapter on "Shaw vs. Shakespeare" (321–39) includes discussion of Shaw's revision of act 5 of *Cym*, which Shaw described as "a tedious string of unsurprising *dénouements* sugared with insincere sentimentality after a ludicrous stage battle" (quoted by Cohn, 335). In chap. 5 (267–309), Cohn discusses the following major 19th- and 20th-century works influenced by *Tmp*: Browning's theologically speculative poem "Caliban upon Setebos" (1864, no. 254); Ernest Renan's philosophical and political plays *Caliban, suite de la Têmpete* (1877) and *L'Eau di Jouvence* (1879); Percy MacKaye's "modern masque" (277) *Caliban by the Yellow Sands* (1916); W. H. Auden's dramatic poem "The Sea and the Mirror" (1944; no. 252); and Aimé Césaire's anti-colonialist play *Une Tempête* (1969; no. 256). For additional commentary on these works, see nos. 255, 265, 267, 270, 272.

F. Pedagogy.

94. Coursen, Herbert R. "Using Film and Television to Teach *The Winter's Tale* and *The Tempest*." In Hunt (no. 95), 117–24.

Coursen analyzes major film and television versions of *WT* and *Tmp*, as well as offshoots such as *Forbidden Planet* (no. 268). Virtually all film and video productions of these plays, Coursen argues, have major limitations. He believes that television lacks sufficient magnitude to provide "an incorporating frame, a sense of the total space" (122) in which action and dialogue take place, and that the television close-up encourages an emphasis on psychological complexity that is less appropriate for the romances than for other works. Coursen notes that engaging students in detailed analysis of different productions encourages questions concerning the impact of the medium and of the historical circumstances of performance.

95. Hunt, Maurice, ed. *Approaches to Teaching Shakespeare's "The Tempest" and Other Late Romances.* Approaches to Teaching World Literature, no. 41. New York: Modern Language Association, 1992.

This volume includes the following essays annotated elsewhere in this volume: Coursen (no. 94), Morse (no. 96), Richmond (no. 97), Waller (no. 98), Young (no. 177), and Peterson (no. 269). Jay Halio (31–37) defends the continuing importance for pedagogy of Tillyard's view (no. 84) of the romances as affirming a harmony that is adumbrated in the later tragedies. Robert F. Willson (38–48) discusses methods of leading students to focus upon metadramatic devices that enhance the audience's sense of the role of art in the process of miraculous regeneration. Michael E. Mooney (49–56) focuses upon Shakespeare's use of "dreams, multiple illusionistic planes, spectacles, music and dance" (50) to create a stylized theatrical form that embodies a vision of renewal and reconciliation. Drawing upon her work in no. 198, Donna Hamilton (64–71) discusses methods of enabling students to appreciate the extent to which artistic language may be informed by the terms of political discourse. Cynthia Lewis (72–79) recommends answering students' objections to *Cym*'s apparent crudity by stressing the play's sophisticated use of such techniques as mirroring devices. Dorothea Kehler (80–86) affirms the importance of addressing the issues of "male domination, sexual guilt, and misogyny" (80) raised by Shakespeare's sympathetic treatment of slandered women in *Cym* and *WT*. Charles R. Forker (94–102) explores ways of leading students to appreciate *WT* as a paradoxical compound of folktale and psychological realism and as a critical analysis of the pastoral tradition. William W. E. Slights (103–8) discusses methods of engaging students in Shakespeare's self-reflexive theater, especially by drawing parallels to postmodern metafiction. Kathleen Campbell (109–16) discusses the value of in-class performance exercises. Kristiaan P. Aercke (146–52) emphasizes illuminating Shakespeare's unresolved questioning of courtly-baroque themes such as dynastic continuity. Emphasizing the prominence of the hypothetical in *Tmp*'s language, Arthur F. Kinney (153–59) describes methods for leading students to explore questions concerning the contingencies of human experience and of interpretation. Kay Stockholder (160–67) recommends a psychoanalytical approach, stressing that Prospero's magic is an image of Shakespeare's art in that it reveals the psychological dynamic behind the effort to "buttress a hierarchical value system" (167). The editor provides discussion of editions of the plays; extensive bibliographical essays on major scholarship and criticism; and an annotated list of audiovisual materials. Hunt's general introduction summarizes many of the teaching practices and critical attitudes of respondents to the MLA survey for this collection. His bibliographical essays are thorough and judicious.

96. Morse, William. "A Metacritical and Historical Approach to *The Winter's Tale* and *The Tempest*." In Hunt (no. 95), 133–38.

Morse provides a new-historicist context for teaching the metacritical aspects of *WT* and *Tmp*. He suggests that the self-reflexivity of Shake-spearean drama, its continual representation of human cognitive power in terms drawn from the stage itself, expresses the Renaissance effort "to valorize the reasoning individual mind as the source of knowledge" (133). Subsequently he explores aspects of the texts that subvert this effort. Throughout this essay, Morse emphasizes the indeterminacy of these works, leading students toward an awareness of "the contingency of meaning in Shakespeare, in literature, in the world" (138).

97. Richmond, Hugh M. "Teaching *The Tempest* and the Late Plays by Performance." In Hunt (no. 95), 124–32.

Richmond argues that involving students in performance is essential in leading them to appreciate the tone of Shakespeare's late plays. By viewing professional performances and by enacting their own, he believes, students experience the detached amusement and "godlike pity for human vicissitude" (129) of these works. Richmond also explains how specific productions and performance techniques illuminate the manner in which "the ritual and the musical choreography of the late Shakespeare make the presence of the transcendental more visible, if less intelligible, than ever before" (131) in Shakespeare's canon.

98. Waller, Gary. "The Late Plays as Family Romance." In Hunt (no. 95), 57–63.

This essay combines psychoanalysis and cultural criticism, exploring the extent to which the dynamics of family relationships are rooted not only in biology but also in specific historical contexts. Waller suggests that the romances are most engaging when they are read in relation to students' own personal histories. He affirms the value of leading students to focus upon the continuities between the family structures typical of our own day and those of the heavily patriarchal culture of the English Renaissance.

G. Collections.

99. Batson, E. Beatrice, ed. *Shakespeare and the Christian Tradition.* Lewiston, N.Y.: Edwin Mellen Press, 1994.

David Bevington's introduction (1–18) proposes that Christian interpretation can benefit from recent literary theory. Bevington uses *Tmp* as one example, assessing both Christian and new historicist interpretations and concluding that "only through the play of ... indeterminacies do values undergo testing" (9). Thomas Howard (163–75) finds that the mixture of tragedy and comedy, implausibility and the marvelous, that occurs in the romances also characterizes Christianity, and he suggests an analogy between the revelations of Shakespearean theater and those of Anglican liturgy.

100. Bloom, Harold, ed. *William Shakespeare: Comedies and Romances.* Modern Critical Views. New York: Chelsea House, 1986.

This anthology reprints the following items annotated elsewhere in this volume: Skura (no. 129), Brower (no. 221), and excerpts from Frye (no. 61) and from chap. 8 of Felperin (no. 58). It also includes Rosalie Colie's discussion of Shakespeare's use of pastoral conventions in *WT* (211–25). Bloom includes a bibliography (295–98) and index (301–6), but he eliminates the original authors' bibliographical notes.

101. Felperin, Howard. *The Uses of the Canon: Elizabethan Literature and Contemporary Theory.* Oxford: Clarendon Press, 1990.

This collection includes four essays by Felperin annotated elsewhere in this volume: nos. 193, 223, 225, 150.

102. Kay, Carol McGinnis, and Henry Jacobs, eds. *Shakespeare's Romances Reconsidered.* Lincoln: Univ. of Nebraska Press, 1978.

This collection begins with Norman Sanders's survey and evaluation (1–10) of major approaches to the romances, concentrating on the 19th and 20th centuries. It includes essays by Hoy (no. 66), Felperin (no. 225), and Young (no. 243), annotated elsewhere in this volume. Northrop Frye (11–39) relates the emphasis on rebirth, resurrection, and visions of ideal order in Shakespeare's romances to the structure of the court masque. In contrast to Frye, Clifford Leech (40–59) interprets Shakespeare's treatment of masques (and unmasking) as ironic commentary on life's pretenses, including the pretense that society can be perfected. Joan Hartwig (91–103) analyzes parody as a means of modulating audience response in the romances. (Hartwig's essay also appears in revised form in her book, *Shakespeare's Analogical Scene: Parody as Structural Syntax*, 171–90, [Lincoln: Univ. of Nebraska Press, 1983].) Joan Warchol Rossi (104–12) discusses Shakespeare's debt to Holinshed, with emphasis on the relation between Britain and Rome. Charles Frey (113–24) emphasizes the tragic intensity of the plot that issues from Leontes' "tyrannical madness" (123) in *WT*. He then comments on the counterplot that leads toward community and brings knowledge of a creative, divinely ordained natural order.

David Bergeron (125–33) connects the renewal of Hermione's life in the statue scene (5.3) to similarly remarkable effects in a civic pageant by Anthony Munday and to Renaissance funerary sculpture. Charles R. Forker (134–48) studies Shakespeare's treatments of art in *The Taming of the Shrew*, *WT*, and *Tmp* in terms of an "implied contrast between celestial and human planes of creativity" (144). The collection concludes with a bibliography (181–215) and index (219–24).

103. Kendall, Gillian Murray, ed. *Shakespearean Power and Punishment: A Volume of Essays.* Madison, N.J.: Fairleigh Dickinson Univ. Press; London: Associated Univ. Presses, 1998.

This collection includes several essays on the romances. Susanne Collier (39–58) compares *Cym* and Beaumont and Fletcher's *Philaster*, emphasizing that both plays undermine feminine power through a ritual sacrifice in which princesses become willing "sacrificial victims" (48); both plays also stress the political dangers of "the seeming indecipherability of women's hearts" (54). Sara Eaton (59–86) discusses "the Lady" in Middleton's *The Second Maiden's Tragedy* and Hermione in *WT* as icons who move the audience to "an acknowledgment of eroticized and violent human weaknesses transcended by ... art" (79–80). Kathryn Barbour (159–72) argues that *Tmp* explores the efficacy and the limitations of Prospero's efforts to maintain power through surveillance, discipline, and punishment. Gillian Murray Kendall's "Overkill in Shakespeare" (173–96) argues that *Measure for Measure*, *Macbeth*, and *WT* dramatize the limits of the power of the state to exact obedience through violence. (A version of this essay appears in *SQ* 43 [1992]: 33–50.) Ronald R. MacDonald (197–209) explores the difficulty of answering the question "Where is the master?" (*Tmp* 1.1.12) as it applies not only to rulers, but also to playwrights (such as Prospero) who strive to control performances of their own plays.

104. Maguire, Nancy Klein, ed. *Renaissance Tragicomedy: Explorations in Genre and Politics.* New York: AMS Press, 1987.

This collection includes several essays relevant to Shakespeare's late plays. The essay by Dixon (no. 31) is annotated elsewhere in this volume. Nancy Klein Maguire's introduction (1–10) and the essays by John T. Shawcross (13–32) and Barbara Mowat (90–96) address problems in defining Renaissance tragicomedy and in applying theories of tragicomedy to Shakespeare's late plays.

105. Muir, Kenneth, ed. *Shakespeare Survey* 29 (1976).

This issue of *Shakespeare Survey* includes the essays by Hoeniger (no.

111) and Siemon (no. 128) annotated elsewhere in this volulme. It also includes Nick Shrimpton's reflections upon directing an academic production of *Tmp* (63–67); Richard Proudfoot's discussion of verbal echoes that unify the two parts of *WT* (67–78); and the essay by Warren cited in the annotation of no. 137. The volume includes an index (187–91).

106. Nicoll, Allardyce, ed. *Shakespeare Survey* 11 (1958).
        This issue of *Shakespeare Survey* includes essays by Edwards (no. 110), Coghill (no. 157), Brockbank (no. 119), and Nosworthy (no. 78) annotated elsewhere in this volume. Clifford Leech (19–30) discusses the relation between dramatic crises and a cyclical concept of time in the romances' five-act structure. C. J. Sisson (70–77) argues that Prospero's magic is predominantly benevolent. The volume includes an index (159–69).

106a. Richards, Jennifer, and James Knowles, eds. *Shakespeare's Late Plays: New Readings.* Edinburgh: Edinburgh Univ. Press, 1999.
        Richards and Knowles's introduction (1–21) surveys the history of scholarship and criticism on the late plays, with emphasis on questions of authorship and the generic coherence of the group. They argue that traditional interpretations of the trajectory of Shakespeare's career depend upon the exclusion or de-emphasis of *The Two Noble Kinsmen* and *Henry VIII*. Helen Hackett (25–39) considers the ways that "maternal imagery" such as "issue" (25) in the late plays suggests that narrative is feminine; yet in all of the late plays except *WT*, she concludes, male characters exert control over authorship. Jennifer Richards (75–91) analyzes *WT*'s treatment of social decorum, concluding that the play questions Leontes' belief that "social distinction exists 'in nature'" (76). Analyzing Prospero's masque (4.1) in the context of a reconsideration of the politics of courtly and aristocratic entertainments, James Knowles (108–25) suggests that "*The Tempest* may ... constructively but critically engage" (124) with royal and aristocratic culture. *Tmp* affirms, in Knowles's reading, that "chastity and virtue" are "achieved states rather than ... inherited gifts" (124). Gareth Roberts (126–42) argues that the magic of *WT* and *Tmp* consists of illusions that evoke wonder but utilize natural powers (including spirits) and therefore are not true miracles; he concludes that such magic is a metaphor for the powers and limitations of human art. William Maley (145–57) explores the manner in which *Cym* fashions British identity and independence as, paradoxically, a replication of the Roman imperial project. For Maley, the return to peace with Rome at the end of *Cym* may be a prophetic symbol of Britain's becoming "more pluralistic, more European, ... more tolerant of religious difference than was Reformation England" (156–57). For

Alison Thorne (176–90), *Cym* explores the ways in which "identity, meaning and value" (179) are dependent on interpretive practices that are unreliable. Thorne argues that the play's emphasis upon acts of misinterpretation leads us not toward fideistic reliance on "divine illumination" (188), but rather toward skepticism. Richard Wilson (193–209) argues that *Double Falsehood*, or *The Distressed Lovers*, published in 1728, is an adaptation of Shakespeare and Fletcher's *Cardenio*. Emphasizing the topicality of the late plays, Wilson discusses Cardenio's protest against the enforced marriage of Frances Howard and the play's hope for religious toleration. Julia Briggs (210–27) comments on the "profound perception of human division and separation" in *Henry VIII* and *The Two Noble Kinsmen*, contrasting these plays' implication that "nothing can be gained without a corresponding loss" (226) with the harmony and optimism of *Tmp*. The volume also contains essays by Margaret Healy on *Pericles*, Gordon McMullan and Thomas Healy on *Henry VIII*, and Alan Stewart on *The Two Noble Kinsmen*.

106b. Ryan, Kiernan, ed. *Shakespeare: The Last Plays.* Longman Critical Readers. London: Longman, 1999.

This collection reprints the following items annotated elsewhere in this volume: Barton (no. 43), Adelman (no. 50), Marcus (no. 121), Felperin (no. 150), Greenblatt (no. 197), Norbrook (no. 235), and extracts from Tennenhouse (no. 39) and Neely (no. 161). Ryan provides an introduction (1–21) to the critical history of the plays and headnotes assessing the contributions of each item.

107. Schwartz, Murray, and Coppélia Kahn, eds. *Representing Shakespeare: New Psychoanalytic Essays.* Baltimore: Johns Hopkins Univ. Press, 1980.

Schwartz and Kahn's introduction (xi–xxi) discusses this volume's essays in the context of developments in literary and psychoanalytical theory. Essays by Kahn (no. 69), Wheeler (no. 87), and Skura (no. 129) are annotated elsewhere in this volume. Schwartz (21–32) discusses the restoration of "masculine identity" and "cultural continuity" in the romances through "restored trust in feminine capacities and the restoration of paternal design of the relationships within which women exist" (30). David Sundelson (33–53), in contrast, argues that *Tmp* univocally affirms a patriarchy so narrow that Sundelson terms it "paternal narcissism" (37). (Sundelson's essay also appears in revised form in *Shakespeare's Restorations of the Father*, 103–21. [New Brunswick: Rutgers Univ. Press, 1983].) David Willbern (264–86) provides "A Bibliography of Psychoanalytic and Psychological Writings on Shakespeare, 1964–1978."

108. Teague, Frances, ed. *Acting Funny: Comic Theory and Practice in Shakespeare's Plays.* Rutherford, N.J.: Fairleigh Dickinson Univ. Press; London: Associated Univ. Presses, 1994.

This collection includes a version of Desmet's essay on *Cym* (see no. 55) annotated elsewhere in this volume. Geraldo U. de Sousa argues that *Tmp* is "less about ... colonialism than about the encounter and interaction of different cultures" (53); he emphasizes parallels between Prospero, as exile and surrogate mother, and Sycorax. Teague's introduction (9–26) discusses the difference between "comedy" and "the comic" and assesses the theories of Frye (no. 60), Susanne Langer, and C. L. Barber.

109. Tobias, Richard C., and Paul G. Zolbrod, eds. *Shakespeare's Late Plays: Essays in Honor of Charles Crow.* Athens: Ohio Univ. Press, 1974.

This collection includes essays by Theresa Coletti (no. 222) and L. C. Knights (no. 231) annotated elsewhere in this volume. Paul G. Zolbrod (1–13) contrasts the tempest imagery of the tragedies (especially *Othello*) and that of the romances; he also contrasts Iago's black magic with Prospero's benign art. Kenneth Muir (32–43) discusses the relation between human action and divine intervention in Shakespearean plays written after 1607. Diana Childress (44–55) argues against applying the term "romance" to Shakespeare's late plays. Leonard Powlick (131–41) argues that *Cym* sustains a comic tone through anticlimactic deflation of pretensions to seriousness. Mike Frank (142–65) argues that *Tmp* lacks the affirmation of providential order found in *Hamlet* and *King Lear*. Gerald Schorin (166–84) uses archetypal analysis of *Tmp*'s plot to examine its complex genre as "tragicomic romance" (182). Elton D. Higgs (200–212) interprets Prospero's art as an imitation of the creative power of God and emphasizes the potential for good and evil in a world whose inhabitants have been granted freedom. Andrew Solomon (213–34) provides commentary on characterization in *Tmp*, emphasizing the play's "vision of a better world" (233).

H. Bibliographies.

110. Edwards, Philip. "Shakespeare's Romances: 1900–1957." *Shakespeare Survey* 11 (1958): 1–18.

Edwards evaluates influential examples of the following general approaches to the romances: biography and the dramatist's spiritual development; sources and influences; myth, symbol, and allegory; the pattern of tragedy and Christian interpretations; and studies of the romance genre.

111. Hoeniger, F. David. "Shakespeare's Romances since 1958: A Retrospect." *Shakespeare Survey* 29 (1976): 1–10.

Hoeniger evaluates major studies in the following categories: theatrical influences, especially coterie theater and the court masque; emblematic and topical interpretations; sources (including prose romances); structure; performance criticism and scholarship; links with Shakespeare's earlier plays; and Northrop Frye, especially *A Natural Perspective* (no. 61).

112. Sajdak, Bruce T., ed. *Shakespeare Index: An Annotated Bibliography of Critical Articles on the Plays, 1959–1983.* 2 vols. Millwood, N.Y.: Kraus International Publications, 1992.

This bibliography is designed to assist readers in locating, "amongst the thousands of possible sources, those few most relevant articles on specific ideas, characters or scenes" (1.xi). Vol. 1, *Citations and Author Index*, includes 12 sections on general topics and genres; 35 sections on individual plays (the three parts of *Henry VI* treated as one play); a section on "Apocrypha" (*The Book of Sir Thomas More, Edward III*, and *The Two Noble Kinsmen*); and an "Author Index" (1.771–801). Chapters in books are not included unless they were published separately as articles. "The Romances" are covered in 1.169–73 (items K1–K36); *Cym* in 1.263–69 (items T1–T56); *WT* in 1.747–63 (items YY1–YY158); and *Tmp* in 1.673–94 (items SS1–SS216). Volume 2, *Character, Scene, and Subject Indexes*, includes a "Character Index" (2.803–1033), with detailed references relating characters to various topics; a "Scene Index" (2.1035–1197), including many subdivisions on aspects of each scene; and an impressively detailed, analytical "Subject Index" (2.1199–1765).

113. Taylor, Michael. "The Late Comedies." In *Shakespeare: A Bibliographical Guide,* new edition, ed. Stanley Wells, 159–79. Oxford: Clarendon Press, 1990.

Taylor's essay surveys and evaluates major 20th-century scholarship and criticism on *Pericles, Cym, WT*, and *Tmp*. He notes that there are relatively few textual problems, and he comments on important editions. The essay includes sections on genre; language and structure; Shakespeare's treatment of the family (including psychoanalytical approaches); connections between psychoanalytical criticism and politics; and treatments of allegory, symbolism, and colonialism in *Tmp*.

See also nos. 58, 70, 95, 102, 107.

III. CYMBELINE

A. Editions.

114. Furness, Horace Howard, ed. *The Tragedie of Cymbeline*. A New Variorum Edition of Shakespeare. Philadelphia: Lippincott, 1913.

In his preface (v–xx), Furness defends *Cym* against detractors such as Samuel Johnson, yet he argues that all parts of the play that breach decorum or verisimilitude must be the work of a "wretched interpolater" (xiv). He also discusses the relationship between *Cym* and Beaumont and Fletcher's *Philaster*, arguing that the latter play was influenced by *Cym*, rather than vice versa. The text is based on the First Folio. Textual notes and extensive commentary from 18th-, 19th-, and early 20th-century scholars and critics appear on each page. The appendix (443–515) discusses date and sources and reprints excerpts of early criticism, much of which is devoted to Imogen as embodiment of ideal feminine virtues. Furness also reprints possible sources; excerpts from Thomas Durfey's 1682 adaptation, *The Injured Princess*; and translations of Shakespeare's songs. Published posthumously, this volume has an index (517–23) but lacks a list of works cited.

115. Maxwell, J. C., ed. *Cymbeline*. Cambridge: Cambridge Univ. Press, 1960.

Maxwell's introduction (xi–xlii) discusses date; authorship (arguing that *Cym* is entirely Shakespearean); sources; and a range of critical issues. Maxwell assesses the relevance of the concept of "tragicomedy" to the play, suggesting that *Cym*'s mixture of comic and tragic moods and its "deliberate incongruity and comic exploitation of conventions" (xxxix) lead to a fairy-tale quality that at times hints at the higher realities of reconciliation and rebirth. He criticizes the "favourite male stereotypes of female character" (xl) that fuel the traditional idealization of Imogen. C. B. Young's stage history (xliii-lv) provides information on productions and a critical survey of adaptations. The text is followed by analysis of the copy for the First Folio (125–28); textual notes and commentary (129–221); and a glossary (222–46).

116. Nosworthy, J. M., ed. *Cymbeline.* The Arden Shakespeare. 1955. Repr., with corrections, London: Methuen; Cambridge: Harvard Univ. Press, 1964. Distributed by Thomas Nelson and sons.

Nosworthy's introduction (xi-lxxxv) discusses the text and authorship (arguing effectively against theories of collaboration or interpolation); date; sources; the possible relation between *Cym* and Beaumont and Fletcher's *Philaster*; and a range of critical topics. Nosworthy sees *Cym* as an experimental romance that uses deliberately fantastic characterization and action in a quest for the golden world with which the play concludes. He discusses the mixture of realism and fantasy in characterization, and he argues that Shakespeare only partially succeeds in his efforts to develop the tragicomic tone and emblematic imagery appropriate for the romance genre. The plot, Nosworthy believes, provides "a full measure of surprise, suspense and wonder" (lxxvi). He discusses the symbolism of the Phoenix in the play's concluding vision of unity, regeneration, and tranquillity. The text is based on the First Folio. Textual notes and extensive commentary appear at the bottom of each page. Appendices (197–224) include reprints of sources; a brief stage history; and discussion of music, with a 17th-century setting for "Hark, Hark, the Lark" (2.3.20–26).

117. Warren, Roger, ed. *Cymbeline.* The Oxford Shakespeare. Oxford: Oxford Univ. Press, 1998.

In his introduction (1–77), Warren emphasizes *Cym*'s sensational theatricality, providing an illustrated history of major productions. He discusses the play's genre; its relation to earlier works in the Shakespeare canon; and its various styles. He analyzes plot and characterization in relation to major sources (especially Boccaccio's *Decameron*), and he evaluates the interpretations of numerous actors and directors, including Peter Hall, William Gaskill, and Adrian Noble. He argues for a probable date of 1610. Warren's analysis of the First Folio text provides convincing evidence against theories of multiple authorship or interpolation. Textual variants and extensive commentary notes appear at the bottom of each page. Appendices (265–76) discuss the spelling of characters' names (notably "Innogen" and "Giacomo"); discuss the role of music in *Cym* and provide James Walker's edition of an early setting, attributed to Robert Johnson, for "Hark, Hark, the Lark"; and record alterations to lineation. The introduction and commentary are thoroughly indexed. See also Warren (no. 137).

B. Authorship; Dating; Textual Studies.

118. Wells, Stanley, and Gary Taylor, with John Jowett and William Montgomery. *William Shakespeare: A Textual Companion.* Oxford: Clarendon Press, 1987.

This book is a companion to *William Shakespeare: The Complete Works* (Oxford: Clarendon Press, 1986; see no. 3.) The authors' discussion of *Cym* in "Canon and Chronology of Shakespeare's Plays" (131–32) argues that the play was influenced by Beaumont and Fletcher's *Philaster* and composed in 1610 (possibly later than *WT*). The later section (604–11) provides detailed textual commentary and argues that the Folio text is based on a transcript by Ralph Crane.

See also nos. 40, 52, 71, 114, 115, 116, 117.

C. Influences; Sources; Intertextuality; Historical and Intellectual Contexts; Topicality.

118a. Boling, Ronald J. "Anglo-Welsh Relations in *Cymbeline*." SQ 51 (2000): 33–66.

This article argues that *Cym* promotes "the English myth of Anglo-Welsh amity" (49). Boling suggests that the early modern Welsh nobility collaborated with England in exchange for political and economic advantages, just as Cymbeline allies himself with Rome in order to solidify his dynasty. In addition, Boling believes, the Roman and British ensigns portrayed together at 5.5.481–82 create the illusion of British equality with Rome, just as "the Welsh dragons on the Tudor coat of arms proclaimed a symbolic equality of the Welsh and English aristocracies" (65). For Boling, Imogen's refinement of the Welshmen dwelling in Belarius's cave suggests the cultural advantages of incorporation into the empire.

119. Brockbank, J. P. "History and Histrionics in Cymbeline." *Shakespeare Survey* 11 (1958): 42–49.

This article argues that studying *Cym*'s sources can help us appreciate Shakespeare's use of "historical romance" (42) to dramatize insights into the forces that have shaped Britain. For Brockbank, *Cym* emphasizes the belief that in order to develop an advanced civilization ancient Britons needed the tutelage of Rome. He also suggests that *Cym*'s conventional histrionics achieve the objectives of the historical romance genre more effectively than more realistic modes. See also Curran (no. 120) and Mikalachki (no. 122).

120. Curran, John E., Jr. "Royalty Unlearned, Honor Untaught: British Savages and Historiographical Change in *Cymbeline*." *Comparative Drama* 3 (1997–98): 277–303.

This article argues that *Cym* is designed to encourage readers to find admirable qualities in ancient Britons despite the fact that the new humanist historiography had discredited the largely mythical, idealized version of history by Geoffrey of Monmouth. For Curran, Guiderius and Arviragus represent "a primitive Britain which is inherently noble despite its savagery" (278), and the characters' virtues are grounded in Nature rather than noble lineage; indeed, the viciousness of the Queen and Cloten is a corollary of their excessive pride in lineage and titles. Curran also argues that the ability to have faith in another's nobility despite his or her shortcomings, a quality embodied in Imogen and learned by Posthumus, is parallel to the ability to admire ancient Britons without idealizing them.

121. Marcus, Leah. *Puzzling Shakespeare: Local Reading and Its Discontents.* Berkeley and Los Angeles: Univ. of California Press, 1988.

Marcus's section on *Cym* (106–48) argues that the play can be read as an allegory supporting James I's advocacy of union between England and Scotland: Jupiter, for example, corresponds to James, and Posthumus to the "Post Nati," those Scotsmen born after James's accession to the throne of England and thus naturalized as citizens of Britain. Yet Marcus also discusses ways that the play deconstructs this reading, especially in certain types of performance; her final conclusion emphasizes the play's potential for instability. An abridged version of this essay appears in *The Historical Renaissance*, ed. Richard Strier and Heather Dubrow, 134–68. Chicago: Univ. of Chicago Press, 1988. The abridged version is reprinted in Ryan (no. 106b).

122. Mikalachki, Jodi. "The Masculine Romance of Roman Britain: *Cymbeline* and Early Modern English Nationalism." *SQ* 46 (1995): 301–22.

Mikalachki interprets *Cym* in the context of a nascent British nationalism that sought to find precedents for masculine civic virtues in connection with the Roman empire; exorcising savagery entailed rejection of ancient British queens such as Boadicea, who once led resistance to Rome, and whose legacy Shakespeare repudiates in his portrait of Cymbeline's evil queen. Mikalachki sees Imogen as "an icon of respectable womanhood" (316) whose praise of Britain contrasts with the evil queen's in that Imogen encourages connections with the larger, civilized Roman world. The essay concludes that Imogen's defining herself through subordinate relations with men reduces the threat of "female autonomy and leadership" (321).

123. Simonds, Peggy Munoz. *Myth, Emblem, and Music and Shakespeare's "Cymbeline": An Iconographic Reconstruction.* Newark: Univ. of Delaware Press; London: Associated Univ. Presses, 1992.

This study seeks to reconstruct a Renaissance *Cym* through study of the play's iconography and its manipulation of conventional topoi. Simonds argues that *Cym* is a Renaissance tragicomedy in its emphasis on personal and social redemption through spiritual love and the aid of providence. She also argues that esoteric symbolism is characteristic of the genre, and she maintains that the myth of Cupid and Psyche as an allegory of the soul's attainment of charity is the play's "inner Neoplatonic idea" (88). The study provides detailed iconographic explications of the following: Imogen's bedchamber as "a Renaissance temple of the graces" and thus "a suitable resting place" (96) for Imogen as embodiment of divine Beauty; Belarius, Arviragus, and Guiderius as primitive wild men who contrast with and ultimately reform a corrupt court; anti-courtier imagery; birds; vegetation; animals; minerals; and rituals. Simonds also discusses the contrast in *Cym* between the deceptions of the corrupt, fallen senses and the final redemption that results from "prayers and music reaching the ears of divinity" and from humans "listening to the resulting good news and responding appropriately to it" (330). She concludes by emphasizing that Neoplatonic-Pythagorean conceptions of cosmic harmony unite the seemingly disparate elements of the play.

See also nos. 114, 115, 116, 117, 118, 124, 125, 127, 130, 131, 138.

D. Language and Linguistics.

See nos. 117, 123, 124, 134.

E. Criticism.

124. Gibbons, Brian. "Fabled *Cymbeline.*" In *Shakespeare and Multiplicity*, 18–47. Cambridge: Cambridge Univ. Press, 1993.

This chapter discusses Shakespeare's transformation of multiple sources in *Cym*, especially Inigo Jones's *Prince Henry's Barriers* and Spenser's *Faerie Queene,* book 2, canto 10. Gibbons argues that Shakespeare presents *Cym* as a fable that combines "myth, recorded fact, legend, folk-tale, romance, his own earlier plays and poems, and miracle" (24) in its account of early British history. Gibbons analyzes unifying imagery (especially jewels and clothing) and analogies among scenes (e.g., 2.2, 4.2, and 5.4), concluding that foreshadowing and other devices enhance the audience's perception of providential forces at work behind the action.

125. Kahn, Coppélia. *Roman Shakespeare: Warriors, Wounds, and Women.* London: Routledge, 1997.

This book argues that Shakespeare criticizes the emulation of Roman exemplars of manly virtue: the wounds that symbolize masculinity simultaneously evoke feminine vulnerability, and the attempt to construct a masculinity "free from the stigma of the feminine" (168) is thus destabilized. The section on *Cym* (160–70) emphasizes the ambivalence of British emulation of Roman virtue. Kahn argues that the play struggles to enable Posthumus to accept "the woman's part" within himself as well as to develop manly virtue.

126. Lawrence, Judiana. "Natural Bonds and Artistic Coherence in *Cymbeline.*" *SQ* 35 (1984): 440–60.

This article analyzes the final act of *Cym*, concluding that it re-establishes the familial and national bonds that provide most of the characters a fulfilling identity and wholeness. The audience, Lawrence argues, views this ending with a double perspective. First, she believes, we share the characters' sense of wonder at the workings of providence; simultaneously, we view the numerous reversals and revelations with an ironic awareness of the artist's display of his ability to provide a fiction that fulfills our longing for harmony.

127. Miola, Robert S. "*Cymbeline*: Beyond Rome." In *Shakespeare's Rome*, 206–35. Cambridge: Cambridge Univ. Press, 1983.

This chapter argues that, in "the best" of *Cym*'s ancient Briton characters, "Roman pride is balanced by humility, Roman courage by the qualities of mercy and forgiveness, Roman constancy by a capacity for flexibility, growth, and change" (207). Miola cites many instances of the play's emphasis on familial love, such as the mysterious affection for Fidele/Imogen expressed by Arviragus and Guiderius, and he praises Posthumus's magnanimous forgiveness of Iachimo as an example of *Cym*'s rejection of the Roman idealization of seeking honor by vanquishing one's enemies. The final union of Rome and Britain, he concludes, is a tribute to the play's exaltation of the value of harmony.

128. Siemon, James Edward. "Noble Virtue in *Cymbeline.*" *Shakespeare Survey* 29 (1976): 51–61.

This article argues that in the first four acts of *Cym* Posthumus is similar to Cloten in his wrathfulness and folly. Siemon analyzes dramatic parallels between the two characters, such as their professions of love and vows of vengeance in 2.3 and 2.4. In act 5, Siemon concludes, Posthumus abandons his concern with external appearances and his erroneous identification of honor with reputation, adopting, as he dons the clothing of a humble Briton, a more genuine understanding of noble virtue.

129. Skura, Meredith. "Interpreting Posthumus's Dream from Above and Below: Families, Psychoanalysts, and Literary Critics." In Schwartz and Kahn (no. 107), 203–16. Repr. in Bloom (no. 100).

Skura discusses the importance of families and family crises in Shakespeare's canon, especially the problem of rebellion of the young against an imprisoning family authority. Posthumus's dream, she believes, is both an epiphany that reveals the role of the gods in human affairs and a liberating revelation of Posthumus's relation to his biological family. Only when he adopts a view of family relations as one in which individuals freely embrace their mutual relationships can Posthumus's marriage to Imogen regain its health. Skura presents this reading as an example of interpretation based on interplay between conscious and unconscious meaning.

130. Swander, Homer. "*Cymbeline* and the 'Blameless Hero.'" *ELH* 31 (1964): 259–70.

This article argues that Shakespeare's characterization of Posthumus is a protest against traditional portrayals of heroes who believe false accusations of their wives' infidelity and yet are held blameless. Swander notes that the ease with which Iachimo deceives Posthumus is underscored by Philario's initial skepticism; he contrasts Posthumus's antifeminist speech at 2.5.1–35 with Imogen's faith in humankind (see, e.g., 3.4.58–64); and he discusses other evidence of *Cym*'s criticism of an "essential meanness in [Posthumus] himself and in the conventional virtue that he embodies" (260). For Swander, Posthumus becomes worthy of Imogen when he confesses his guilt and rejects the false morality that he previously embodied; Shakespeare thus criticizes "accepted ideas about the kind of insights that love demands and provides" (269).

131. Turner, Robert Y. "Slander in *Cymbeline* and Other Jacobean Tragicomedies." *English Literary Renaissance* 13 (1983): 182–202.

This essay interprets *Cym* in the context of a reaction against satire and detraction that occurred in the early 1600s. The article suggests that, although this reaction is due in part to "legal controversies aroused by topical indiscretions" (184), it often took the form of assessing slander as uncharitable. Turner contrasts the cynicism of Iachimo, Posthumus, and

Cymbeline (in his distrust of Belarius) with the faith that sustains the slandered Imogen/Fidele. He concludes that both the miraculous intervention of Jupiter and the form of the play's denouement suggest the limitations of human knowledge and thus commend "the [ostensibly] impractical outlook of trust and hope in the face of contrary evidence" (202).

F. Stage History; Performance Criticism; Film and Television Versions.

132. Granville-Barker, Harley. *Prefaces to Shakespeare: Cymbeline.* Revised edition. In *Prefaces to Shakespeare.* Vol. 2, *King Lear, Cymbeline, Julius Caesar,* 75–159. Princeton: Princeton Univ. Press, 1946. Repr. 1963.

Granville-Barker argues that the "frankly informative" (79) soliloquies of *Cym* are one aspect of the play's "sophisticated artlessness, the art that rather displays art rather than conceals it" (81–82). Similarly, he describes the elaborate complications and resolutions of the multiple plots as an "exhibition of tricks" (83) designed to display the playwright's skill. He suggests that the play's use of conscious anachronism and its theophany in 5.4 contribute to an aura of fantasy, and he recommends costuming and set design that will hover between "realism and illusion" (98). In his commentary on characters, Granville-Barker describes Iachimo as a villain who loves evil purely for the sport of it; Posthumus as a man whose credulity is a weak foundation for moral character and who attains genuine faith when he is forgiven for his transgressions; and Imogen as "a pleasantly human paragon" who displays "chastity, faith, fidelity" (146). See also Lawrence (no. 126), Kirsch (no. 134), and Warren (no. 137).

133. Jacobs, Henry. "Rewriting Shakespeare: The Framing of *Cymbeline.*" *Renaissance Papers 1983,* ed. A. Leigh DeNeef and M. Thomas Hester, associate ed. Joseph A. Porter, 79–87. Raleigh, N.C.: Southeastern Renaissance Conference, 1983.

Jacobs discusses framing devices used by modern directors to impose on *Cym* a coherence that appears to be lacking in Shakespeare's text. He points out that directors often use an "inductor" or "mediating fiction" (83) to provide commentary on the action or to influence audience response. The essay concludes that all of these devices are efforts "to repair what is perceived as a deeply flawed play" (86). The final effect, Jacobs believes, is an inappropriate reduction of the dissonance and ambiguity inherent in Shakespearean tragicomedy.

134. Kirsch, Arthur C. "*Cymbeline* and Coterie Dramaturgy." *ELH* 34 (1967): 288–306. Repr. in *Shakespeare's Later Comedies*, ed. D. J. Palmer. Penguin Shakespeare Library. Harmondsworth: Penguin, 1971.

This article analyzes the dramaturgy associated with Blackfriars theater and its aristocratic audience and developed by John Marston, Francis Beaumont and John Fletcher, and Shakespeare. Drawing on Granville-Barker (no. 132), Kirsch emphasizes self-conscious artistry that calls attention to the dramatist's technique; discontinuities in characterization and plot and an emphasis upon "declamatory displays" (289); devices that create a mixture of audience engagement and detachment; and "sensationally mingled tones in tragicomedy" (291). In *Cym*, Kirsch argues, Shakespeare adapted this dramaturgy to his own purposes, establishing "a pattern of action profoundly concerned with rebirth, regeneration, and redemption through suffering made intelligible through the Christian idea of the fortunate fall" (298). Kirsch relates the theme of the fortunate fall to the prevalence of paradox in the play's language and to "a conflation of emotions resulting in wonder" (302).

135. Moshinsky, Elijah, director. Shaun Sutton, producer. *Cymbeline*. The BBC "Shakespeare Plays" Series, 1982.

Although this television version has been credited with preserving more of Shakespeare's text than other productions, Moshinsky nonetheless makes significant cuts and reorders scenes and sections, apparently in an effort to simplify *Cym*'s complex plot. The setting and costumes are Jacobean. Performances by David Creedon (Arviragus), Michael Gough (Belarius), Paul Jesson (Cloten), Richard Johnson (Cymbeline), Geoffrey Burridge (Guiderius), Robert Lindsay (Iachimo), Helen Mirren (Imogen), Michael Pennington (Posthumus), Claire Bloom (Queen), and others have been well received. Available from Time-Life Video; The Writing Company; and elsewhere. For additional information and commentary, see Rothwell and Melzer (no. 24), item 73.

136. Walter, Harriet. "Imogen." In *Players of Shakespeare 3: Further Essays in Shakespeare Performance by Players with the Royal Shakespeare Company*, 201–19. Ed. Russell Jackson and Robert Smallwood. Cambridge: Cambridge Univ. Press, 1993.

In describing her development of the role of Imogen for the 1987 RSC production (directed by Bill Alexander), Walter insists upon the inadequacy of interpreting Imogen as an incarnation of perfect virtue. She emphasizes that Imogen asserts her integrity with sufficient impulsiveness and rebelliousness to embark on a forbidden marriage. Walter stresses Imogen's volatility and the mixture of love and anger in her relations with both Cymbeline and Posthumus. See also Warren (no. 137).

137. Warren, Roger. *Cymbeline.* Shakespeare in Performance. General eds. J. R. Mulryne and J. C. Bulman. Manchester: Manchester Univ. Press, 1989. Distributed in the U. S. and Canada by St. Martin's Press.

This study stresses *Cym*'s capacity to "astonish and to move an audience" through "theatrical virtuosity" and "language of exceptional evocative power" (1). In his survey of the play's reception and performance history (1–26), Warren stresses *Cym*'s Ovidian interest in extreme states of emotion, and he argues that the play's much discussed self-conscious artifice (see Lawrence [no. 126], Granville-Barker [no. 132], and Kirsch [no. 134]) intensifies our interest in the characters' experience, rather than distancing us. Drawing upon reviews, statements by actors and directors, and other records, Warren provides detailed analysis of performances directed by Peter Hall at Stratford-upon-Avon in 1957 and at the National Theatre in 1988; William Gaskill's 1962 production at Stratford with Vanessa Redgrave, Eric Porter, and Patrick Allen; Elijah Moshinsky's television adaptation, 1982 (no. 135); productions by Jean Gascon (1970) and Robin Phillips (1986) at the Festival Theatre at Stratford, Ontario; and Bill Alexander's production with Harriet Walter (see Walter [no. 136]) at The Other Place in Stratford-upon-Avon (1987). Warren combines literary and theatrical criticism to illuminate a range of interpretive issues, especially with regard to characterization and the play's emotional impact on audiences. This book expands aspects of Warren's commentary in "Theatrical Virtuosity and Poetic Complexity in *Cymbeline*," *Shakespeare Survey* 29 (1976): 41–49.

See also nos. 115, 117.

G. *Reception History; Adaptations;* Cymbeline *as Source for and Influence on Later Writers and Works.*

See nos. 93, 114, 116, 133.

H. *Collections.*

138. Gillies, John, and Virginia Mason Vaughan, eds. *Playing the Globe: Genre and Geography in English Renaissance Drama.* Madison, N.J.: Fairleigh Dickinson Univ. Press; London: Associated Univ. Presses, 1998.

This collection includes two essays on *Cym*. Rhonda Lemke Sanford (63–85) interprets the play in the context of the Renaissance practice of representing lands as feminine and conquerors or cartographers as masculine; she concludes that the play's denouement depicts Imogen as a conquered possession. Glenn Clark (230–59) argues that *Cym* defends the orthodox conceptions of natural and geopolitical order that James I affirmed in his arguments for unification of Scotland and England.

I. Bibliographies.

139. Jacobs, Henry. *Cymbeline.* The Garland Shakespeare Bibliographies, no. 3. New York: Garland, 1982.

Jacobs's goal is to annotate all scholarship and criticism on *Cym* published between 1940–80, plus major previous contributions. He includes over 1,400 items organized into eight categories: criticism (including authorship); sources; dating; textual studies; bibliographies; editions; productions and stage history; and translations, adaptations, influence, and synopses. Jacobs's introduction (xv–xlviii) surveys and evaluates major work in each of these areas. There is a comprehensive index (539–91).

See also nos. 95, 110, 111, 112, 113.

IV. THE WINTER'S TALE

A. Editions.

140. Furness, Horace Howard, ed. *The Winter's Tale.* A New Variorum Edition of Shakespeare. Philadelphia: Lippincott, 1898. Repr. New York: American Scholar Publications, 1966.

In his preface (v–xiii) Furness discusses the general plan of the New Variorum; *WT*'s text; and Garrick's adaptation, *Florizel and Perdita.* The text is based on the First Folio. Textual notes and extensive commentary from 18th- and 19th- century scholars and critics appear on each page. The appendix (307–423) surveys scholarship on the text; date; sources (including a reprint of Greene's *Pandosto*); and a number of critical issues, including characterization and Shakespeare's disregard for the unities of time, place, and action. Furness reprints excerpts of criticism by F. J. Furnivall, S. T. Coleridge, A. W. Schlegel, and many others. He reprints two 17th-century settings for songs and includes commentary on 18th- and 19th-century performances. The "Plan of the Work" (417–23) includes a partial list of works cited. The volume concludes with an index (425–32), and the 1966 reprint includes (I–XVII) Louis Marder's *The Winter's Tale: A Supplementary Bibliography* (1898–1965).

141. Kermode, Frank, ed. *The Winter's Tale.* Signet Classic Shakespeare. Newly revised edition. New York: Penguin Putnam, 1998.

Kermode's introduction (lxiii–lxxvii) discusses versification, imagery, theological elements, plot, and characters in the context of *WT*'s dramatization of the healing power of time and "great creating Nature." Human art, he argues, is subsumed within the divinely sanctioned natural order. The text, based on the First Folio, is followed (117–18) by a textual note and a list of emendations. Annotation appears at the bottom of each page. The major source, Greene's *Pandosto*, is discussed and partially reprinted (119–41). This edition reprints (143–91) excerpts from criticism by S. Forman, S. T. Coleridge, E.M.W. Tillyard, G. W. Knight, Carol Thomas Neely (no. 161), and Coppélia Kahn. Sylvan Barnet's essay, "*The Winter's Tale* on Stage and Screen" appears on 193–207. The volume concludes with a selected bibliography (209–22). For annotation of the general editor's contributions, see no. 5.

142. Orgel, Stephen, ed. *The Winter's Tale.* The Oxford Shakespeare. Oxford: Oxford Univ. Press, 1996.

Orgel's introduction (1–83) discusses problems of genre and verisimilitude; the linguistic indeterminacy of many passages; *WT*'s responses to patriarchy and royal absolutism (concluding that the play ultimately affirms a patriarchal social order); the characterization of Leontes, Hermione, Paulina, and Autolycus; nature and art; "the interrelationships of art, magic, religion, and theatre" (61); and date and text. The illustrated section on theater history (62–77) focuses upon the final scene (5.3). Textual notes and commentary appear at the bottom of each page. Appendices (233–83) reprint Simon Forman's account of a performance in 1611; Greene's *Pandosto,* the major source; and four 17th-century settings for songs. The introduction, commentary, and appendices are indexed (285–95).

143. Pafford, J.H.P., ed. *The Winter's Tale.* The Arden Shakespeare. London: Methuen; Cambridge: Harvard Univ. Press, 1963.

Pafford's introduction (xv–lxxxix) discusses the text (based on the First Folio); date and authorship (persuasively rejecting theories of collaboration or interpolation); sources; and a range of critical issues. After a survey of criticism on the romances, Pafford concludes that the happy endings result from human love and constancy aided by the gods. He argues that in *WT* Shakespeare renders a fairy-tale plot believable, and he comments on the mixture of realism and thematic convention in characterization. Pafford relates the play's style to characterization and the demands of performance. Textual notes and commentary appear at the bottom of each page. Appendices (163–225) contain miscellaneous longer notes; a discussion of music; a brief stage history; and a reprint of Greene's *Pandosto.*

144. Schanzer, Ernest, ed. *The Winter's Tale.* New Penguin Shakespeare. Harmondsworth, England: Penguin, 1969.

Schanzer's introduction (7–46) explores the means through which Shakespeare intensifies the audience's sense of wonder at Hermione's reappearance. It also discusses characterization, the relation between *WT* and Greene's *Pandosto,* and the parallels and contrasts between the two halves of the play. Schanzer concludes that, although the contrasts emphasize the change from winter and desolation to spring and rebirth, the parallels suggest that human fortunes are as cyclical as the seasons. Schanzer argues that *WT*'s stature derives from the sophistication of its structure, characterization, and poetry, rather than from profundity of theme or symbolism. He provides a brief, selected bibliography (47–48). The text is based on the First Folio. The text is followed by textual notes and commentary (161–233); an account of the First Folio and a textual collation (235–39); and early settings for three songs.

B. Authorship; Dating; Textual Studies.

145. Wells, Stanley, and Gary Taylor, with John Jowett and William Montgomery. *William Shakespeare: A Textual Companion.* Oxford: Clarendon Press, 1987.

This book is a companion to *William Shakespeare: The Complete Works* (Oxford: Clarendon Press, 1986; see no. 3.) The authors' discussion of *WT* in "Canon and Chronology of Shakespeare's Plays" (131) argues for a date of 1609 (possibly earlier than *Cym*). The later section (601–3) provides detailed textual commentary and argues that the Folio text is based on a transcript by Ralph Crane.

See also nos. 40, 52, 140, 142, 143.

C. Influences; Sources; Intertextuality; Historical and Intellectual Contexts; Topicality.

146. Barkan, Leonard. "'Living Sculptures': Ovid, Michelangelo, and *The Winter's Tale.*" *ELH* 48 (1981): 639–67. Excerpt repr., in revised form, in *The Gods Made Flesh*, 283–88. New Haven: Yale Univ. Press, 1986.

This article interprets *WT*'s statue scene (5.3) in the context of classical and Renaissance stories of statues that come to life. Barkan discusses works and aesthetic theories of Ovid (including the story of Pygmalion), Michelangelo, Giulio Romano (as described in Giorgio Vasari's *Lives of the Artists*), and others. He concludes that the scene simultaneously celebrates the power of art to "crystallize a true essence, whether of life, of art, or of love" (664) and the power of love and faith (and hence Nature) to bring life to Hermione, whose existence had been rendered barren by Leontes' jealousy.

147. Mowat, Barbara A. "Rogues, Shepherds, and the Counterfeit Distressed: Texts and Infracontexts of *The Winter's Tale* 4.3." *Shakespeare Studies* 22 (1994): 58–76.

Mowat explores the ways in which the meanings of *WT* 4.3 are enriched by awareness of "infracontexts, some of which supplement and intensify each other, while others set up sharply contrasting associations and patterns" (59). Mowat notes that Autolycus has often been read as an embodiment of the "trickster" archetype associated with Mercury; he can also be understood in relation to texts that call for punishment of rogues who pretend infirmity and live by begging and thievery. She emphasizes, however, that many texts (including More's *Utopia*) recognize the origin of poverty in enclosures that dispossess laborers. Mowat suggests that an understanding of the resemblance between 4.3 and the parable of the Good Samaritan and of conflicting social attitudes toward beggars and shepherds can enrich our experience of the power of this scene.

147a. Nuttall, A. D. "*The Winter's Tale*: Ovid Transformed." In *Shakespeare's Ovid*, ed. A. D. Taylor, 135–49. Cambridge: Cambridge Univ. Press, 2000.

Focusing upon the sheep-shearing scene (4.4.) and the statue scene (5.3), Nuttall discusses Shakespeare's transformation of the stories of Proserpina, Orpheus, and Pygmalion. He contrasts Ovid's "strangely hard playfulness" with Shakespeare's "serious beauty, not only light but also a sudden astonishing warmth" (141–42). The essay concludes that Shakespeare's artistic evocation of the apparently miraculous stimulates wonder at the fully natural: in contrast to recent attempts to argue that "what seems to be real may be constituted by convention," Shakespeare's art persuades us that "within the most wantonly theatrical episode, truth might still be operative" (147).

148. Paster, Gail Kern. *The Body Embarrassed: Drama and the Disciplines of Shame in Early Modern England.* Ithaca: Cornell Univ. Press, 1993.

This book's section on *WT* (260–80) argues that Leontes' rage in act 1 is based on a psychologically regressive competition with Polixenes for the nurture of the maternal body represented by the pregnant Hermione, and that the king's persecution of his wife is an effort to exert patriarchal control over female reproductive power. Paster also interprets Perdita's abrupt separation from her mother as a heightened reflection of anxieties produced by the practice of entrusting aristocratic or royal infants to wet nurses from the lower classes. Paster suggests that Perdita's experience "becomes the sign that the child who went out is the child who returns, unchanged in the essentials of bearing and grace that identify her as a 'natural' member of the ruling class" (276). Unlike those such as Neely (no. 161) who argue that *WT*'s final scene suggests acceptance of female sexuality, Paster concludes that as a "living statue" who embraces Leontes in silence, Hermione is "visibly altered and diminished by her experience of patriarchal discipline" (278–79).

See also nos. 40, 52, 140, 141, 142, 143, 144, 149,
165, 168, 169, 172, 176, 180.

D. Language and Linguistics.

149. Enterline, Lynn. " 'You Speak a Language That I Understand Not': The Rhetoric of Animation in *The Winter's Tale.*" *SQ* 48 (1997): 17–44.

This article maintains that *WT* questions the belief embodied in Ovidian and Petrarchan traditions that powerful masculine speech depends upon "female absence or resistance" (23): Leontes must learn that "power resides only fleetingly in one's voice, even if it be the voice of a poet or a king" (28). Enterline stresses that Paulina, whose voice cannot be silenced, cures Leontes; in the final scene (5.3) Paulina's power is related to the story of Pygmalion, a fantasy of the ability of language to animate a statue. Enterline also emphasizes that in 5.3 Hermione does not speak to Leontes, whose jealousy was grounded in fear of his wife's "superior rhetorical skill" (18); she instead expresses maternal concern for a lost child whom the play compares to Proserpina. Enterline thus compares Hermione to Ceres, who expresses grief over violence to women in Ovidian mythology. A revised version of this article appears as chap. 6 (198–226) of Enterline's *The Rhetoric of the Body from Ovid to Shakespeare* (Cambridge: Cambridge Univ. Press, 2000).

150. Felperin, Howard. " 'Tongue-Tied Our Queen?': The Deconstruction of Presence in *The Winter's Tale.*" In *Shakespeare and the Question of Theory*, ed. Patricia Parker and Geoffrey Hartman, 3–18. New York: Methuen, 1985. Repr., with revisions, in Felperin (no. 101) and Ryan (no. 106b).

This essay initially asks whether there could be any grounds for Leontes' jealousy, and it subsequently focuses on *WT*'s linguistic indeterminacy. Even the truth of the oracle of Apollo, Felperin suggests, can be questioned. Yet he concludes that the uncertainty of language, the limitations of its powers of representation, can lead not only to the jealousy of act 1, but also to the faith invoked by Paulina at *WT*'s conclusion. For commentary, see Bennett (no. 154).

151. Gourlay, Patricia A. " 'O My Most Sacred Lady': Female Metaphor in *The Winter's Tale.*" *English Literary Renaissance* 5 (1975): 375–95. Repr. in Hunt (no. 179).

This article argues that the language of *WT* confers a mythical status

upon Hermione, Paulina, and Perdita, associating them with the benevolent power of "love, art and nature" (377). Gourlay contrasts the quasi-re-
ligious terms applied to these women with Leontes' diction in the early
acts, which suggests that his jealousy is grounded in fear of sexuality and
in materialism; at 1.1.203, for example, he refers to Hermione as merely
another female "belly" (379). For Gourlay, Hermione is associated with
the celestial Venus of the Neoplatonic tradition and with Grace; Perdita,
whom Leontes calls a "goddess" (5.1.131), embodies the creative power of
Venus Genetrix. Gourlay concludes that the power of "grace and fertili-
ty" (394) associated with these female characters transforms the sterile
social order of the play.

152. McDonald, Russ. "Poetry and Plot in *The Winter's Tale.*" *SQ* 36
(1985): 315–29. Repr. in Hunt (no. 179).

    This article argues that poetic and rhetorical style in *WT* parallel tragi-
comic structure in the plot. McDonald finds a periodic structure in the
syntax of many passages, the final meaning disclosed only at the end. Both
the plot and the poetry thus lead us to experience complex mysteries that,
if we are patient, are resolved in a final revelation.

152a. McKeown, Adam. "Rhetoric and the Tragedy of *The Winter's Tale.*"
The Upstart Crow 20 (2000): 116–32.

    This article argues that the tragedy enacted in the first three acts of
WT is "dominated by rhetoric" (116). Though McKeown does not claim
to clarify fully the basis of Leontes' jealousy, he emphasizes that Leontes
is threatened by Hermione's ability to persuade Polixenes to remain in
Sicilia. For McKeown, Leontes shares the faith of Renaissance humanists
in the ability of the orator to establish moral order, yet the play repeated-
ly dramatizes "the failure of rhetoric to lead to understanding or promote
cohesion among people" (124). Instead, this essay concludes, *WT* demonstrates that "people's minds are most profoundly moved not when they
are persuaded, but when they are confronted with something beyond
words" (129); the play's resolution thus depends upon "visual wonders"
(129) such as the apparent vivification of Hermione's statue in 5.3.

See also nos. 141, 142, 143, 144, 154, 155, 159,
162, 166, 171, 172, 179, 180.

E. Criticism.

153. Barber, C. L. " 'Thou That Beget'st Him That Did Thee Beget': Transformation in *Pericles* and *The Winter's Tale*." *Shakespeare Survey* 22 (1969): 59–67.

This psychoanalytical essay argues that the resolutions of *Pericles* and *WT* derive from the transformation of love through purgation of fear of "gross sexuality" (66), including latent homosexuality or incest. Love, Barber concludes, is thus revealed to be the force that links human action to the sacred generative powers of the cosmos. The essay discusses the power of Shakespearean poetry and stagecraft to create an aura of sanctification around characters such as Hermione. This article provides a concise, early version of the theory developed in Barber and Wheeler (no. 51).

154. Bennett, Kenneth C. "Reconstructing *The Winter's Tale*." *Shakespeare Survey* 46 (for 1993): 81–90.

Responding to Felperin (no. 150) and to Joyce Wexler's "A Wife Lost and/or Found," *The Upstart Crow* 8 (1988): 106–17, Bennett argues that deconstructive readings of *WT* are implausible, especially in light of literary and theatrical conventions that guide audience response. He maintains, for example, that commentary by minor characters whom we have no reason to disbelieve confirms our faith in Hermione's innocence and the truth of the oracle. Bennett also argues that failure to maintain faith in Hermione would make the play's conclusion intolerable. Stressing the various types of thematic, structural, or affective unity that texts are found to possess, Bennett concludes that "the deconstructive nature of language and utterance is countered by an inevitable tendency to construct and to reconstruct" (90).

155. Bethell, S. L. "*The Winter's Tale*": A Study. London: Staples Press [1947]. Repr. Folcroft, Pa.: Folcroft, 1974, and n.p.: Norwood Editions, 1978. Excerpt repr. in Muir (no. 180).

Bethell's introduction (9–14) argues that Shakespeare's plays are a compound of "conventionalism and naturalism" (9) and that their "interpretation of life ... is ... profoundly Christian" (14). Part 1 (17–67) analyzes *WT*'s verse, its romance plot and setting, and its treatment of time, all in relation to the play's emphasis on redemption and its suggestion that one can sense the interpenetration of a supernatural order into "the natural affections, social sanctions, and other manifestations of the natural order" (30). Bethell argues that conscious anachronism and a mixture of the real and the mythological contribute to a fusion of "the remote and

..r, the ancient and the modern, in a statement of eternal truth ..scending time and place" (31). This section also discusses the ways in which *WT* calls attention to itself as a play, suggests the relation between different "planes of reality," and thus suggests "the relativity even of that plane upon which the audience find themselves" (58). Part 2 (71–104) analyzes the manner in which the play's imagery and symbolism suggest that a theology of sin, repentance, and providential redemption are immanent in *WT*'s story. He focuses, for example, on the numerous references to "grace" and the Old Shepherd's line, "Now bless thyself: thou mettest with things dying, I with things new-born" (3.3.112–14), and he argues that the play's conclusion dramatizes the regeneration of a corrupt court through infusion of the "rural virtues" (94) and vitality associated with pastoral. Bethell emphasizes the distinction between Shakespeare's subtle and oblique artistic methods and those of allegory. The conclusion (107–18) relates Shakespeare's synthesis of the sacred and the secular and his vision of the possibility of spiritually pure sexual love to Christian humanism.

156. Bishop, T. G. *Shakespeare and the Theatre of Wonder.* Cambridge: Cambridge Univ. Press, 1996.

This book discusses wonder as a product of the relation between fiction and reality, the possible and the impossible. The section on *WT* (125–75) comments on the relation between the horror story Mamillius begins in 2.1 and the actual tale of Leontes' terrifying jealousy. Bishop emphasizes Leontes' fear of sexuality and his projection of his own guilt onto Hermione. Leontes constructs a "pageant of calumny" (146), Bishop continues, that contrasts with Dion and Cleomenes' play of absolute knowledge and Paulina's drama of penance. Ultimately, this book argues, the psychology and aesthetic of *WT* are grounded in the myth of Proserpine: Leontes corresponds to Dis, whose desire produces wintry death, yet the Bohemian pastoral reveals human desire's connection to natural fecundity and renewal. The chapter concludes with a complex meditation on the statue scene (5.3) as a study in the relation between life and art: Leontes must regard Hermione's "statue" with the fully engaged attention that constitutes love before she can come to life. The wonder of the final scene, Bishop concludes, derives in part from its balance between suggestions of transcendence and its affirmation of the renewal of physical life.

157. Coghill, Nevill. "Six Points of Stage-Craft in *The Winter's Tale.*" *Shakespeare Survey* 11 (1958): 31–41. Repr. in Muir (no. 180).

Coghill discusses six aspects of *WT* frequently regarded as weaknesses of the play: Leontes's supposedly sudden jealousy (1.2); the unexpected bear that devours Antigonus (3.3); Father Time (4.1); "the crude shifts to clear stage in the Florizel-Perdita-Camillo-Autolycus scene" (36); the narration in 5.2 concerning the meeting of Leontes, Polixenes, Perdita, and Florizel; and the statue scene (5.3). In each instance, Coghill argues, the events in question skillfully advance the structure and meaning of the play and evoke appropriate audience response. Most impressive is his argument that the bear and the clown's discussion of Antigonus's death are a blend of tragedy and comedy that provides a skillful transition between the predominantly tragic and the predominantly comic parts of the play. For commentary, see Matchett (no. 160).

158. Erickson, Peter. "The Limitations of Reformed Masculinity in *The Winter's Tale*." In *Patriarchal Structures in Shakespeare's Drama.* Chap. 5, 148–72. Berkeley and Los Angeles: Univ. of California Press, 1985.

This essay argues that *WT* dramatizes a "transition from a brutal, crude, tyrannical version [of patriarchy] to a benevolent one capable of ... valuing women" (148). Erickson emphasizes that Leontes' jealousy springs from his awareness that Hermione possesses greater power to influence Polixenes than Leontes does. At the end of the play the male power structure has been purged of this excessive fear of women, but Hermione, Perdita, and Paulina, despite their resistance of tyranny, all remain subordinate to reformed male authority. For Erickson, women are valued in *WT* because they nurture and forgive men, and Shakespeare portrays this construction of gender relations as natural and benevolent. An earlier version of this essay appeared as "Patriarchal Structures in *The Winter's Tale*," *PMLA* 97 (1982): 819–29. See also Bergeron (no. 29), Adelman (no. 50) and Barber and Wheeler (no. 51).

159. Knights, L. C. "'Integration' in *The Winter's Tale*." *Sewanee Review* 84 (1976): 595–613. Repr. in Bloom (no. 178).

Knights contrasts the psychic disorder reflected in Leontes' lines at 1.2.128–46 with the health and vitality of Florizel's speech at 4.4.135–46. He then explores the ways in which *WT*'s action and poetry lead us from "self-enclosure" and "chaos" to "a grace of human living, felt intensely in an individual presence, but related ... to impersonal forces of generation" (606). The play moves us, Knights believes, toward the experience of "integration," understood as both psychic wholeness and healthy relation to humankind and the natural order. This essay combines sensitive formalist analysis with discreet use of psychoanalytical concepts.

60. **Matchett, William H.** "Some Dramatic Techniques in *The Winter's Tale.*" *Shakespeare Survey* 22 (1969): 93–107.

Responding to Coghill (no. 157), this essay analyzes three scenes in *WT*, in each instance seeking to reveal sophisticated techniques that previous critics have missed. Through explication of the dialogue in 1.1, Matchett argues that Leontes' jealousy evolves gradually and plausibly. He then argues that 3.3, in which Antigonus's being devoured by a bear is juxtaposed to an affirmation of new life embodied in the infant Perdita, leads us to "question our own responses" (102) to the play's mixture of tragedy and comedy. Matchett concludes by arguing that the effective dramatic suspense, stage action, and formal structure of the statue scene (5.3) convince us that art can reveal "a miracle in the full effect of which we participate" (103).

161. **Neely, Carol Thomas.** "Women and Issue in *The Winter's Tale.*" *Philological Quarterly* 57 (1978): 181–94. Expanded in *Broken Nuptials in Shakespeare's Plays*, 166–209. New Haven: Yale Univ. Press, 1985. Repr. in Bloom (no. 178); extract from *Broken Nuptials* repr. in Ryan (no. 106b).

This article argues that Hermione, Paulina, and Perdita are more fully developed and active than women of other romances, and through speech and action they bring the male characters to healthy acceptance of "sexuality and childbirth, separation and change, growth and decay" (*PQ*, 181). For Neely, Hermione's appearance in Antigonus's vision gives her a role analogous to those of the gods in *Pericles* and *Cym*; Paulina is Hermione's priestess, and the transformation of a statue into a living woman in the final scene symbolizes Leontes' acceptance of his wife as flesh and blood. The expanded version in *Broken Nuptials* places this argument in the context of further commentary on conflicting attitudes toward sexuality and patriarchy in the romances.

162. **Nuttall, A. D.** *William Shakespeare: "The Winter's Tale."* Studies in English Literature, ed. David Daiches, no. 26. London: Edward Arnold, 1966.

Nuttall argues that while the romances contain "mythic reverberation" (11), such as an association of Hermione with Alcestis, we should not reduce the characters to allegorical symbols. He provides close readings of language in relation to psychoanalytical interpretations of character; he relates Leontes' jealousy, for example, to repressed sexual guilt. He then contrasts the analysis of guilt of the first two acts in Sicily with the complex innocence of Bohemia. His account of the final act focuses upon the relation of the "improbable-realistic" (58) to the play's evocation of the miraculous. Throughout this brief book, Nuttall argues that *WT* evokes a sense of the divine without consistently drawing upon Christian doctrine.

163. Overton, Bill. *The Winter's Tale.* The Critics' Debate. General ed. Michael Scott. Atlantic Highlands, N.J: Humanities Press, 1989.

After the introductory discussion (9–12) of Overton's pluralist methodology, part 1 of this book (13–53) provides a critical survey of approaches to *WT* in the contexts of performance history and the presuppositions of modern literary studies. Part 2 (55–85) discusses *WT*'s theatricality, its analysis of "the dangers of absolute power" (60), and its critique of Leontes' and Polixenes' unhealthy distrust of women. Overton argues that *WT* evokes unorthodox responses to social stereotypes and received political assumptions; we are led to admire Paulina, for example, whom Leontes initially labels as a shrew and a witch. Yet the play's fairy-tale atmosphere, its wit and paradox, Overton adds, might permit orthodox viewers (such as James I) to perceive the play as innocuous.

164. Palmer, Daryl W. "Jacobean Muscovites: Winter, Tyranny, and Knowledge in *The Winter's Tale.*" SQ 46 (1995): 323–39.

This essay discusses the significance of *WT*'s allusions to Muscovite tyranny and violence: examples include Hermione's reference to her father, "the Emperor of Russia" (3.2.119); the bear that devours Antigonus in 3.3; and Autolycus's description of "authority" as a "stubborn bear" (4.3.801-2). Palmer also connects characters' concealment of knowledge to quests for power. He concludes that the romance's happy ending derives from Leontes's abandonment of secrecy and suspicion and his embracing communal knowledge of his injustice.

165. Pyle, Fitzroy. *"The Winter's Tale": A Commentary on the Structure.* London: Routledge and Kegan Paul; New York: Barnes and Noble, 1969.

This book provides scene-by-scene analysis of *WT*, commenting on dialogue, plot structure, characterization, and implied stage action. Pyle argues that the play possesses organic form, and he seeks to demonstrate that every scene enhances the work's unity and illustrates Shakespeare's skillful manipulation of audience response. For Pyle, everything in *WT* prepares us for the restoration of Hermione, an event that "represents the miraculous power of the human spirit, rightly directed [by the gods], to achieve the impossible" (8). Pyle frequently seeks clues to Shakespeare's artistic purposes through analysis of his transformation of Greene's *Pandosto*, the play's major source. He considers the possible influence of

Blackfriars theater on the style of the last plays and argues that "tragicomic romance" is the most useful generic description of them.

166. Sanders, Wilbur. *The Winter's Tale.* Twayne's New Critical Introductions to Shakespeare. Boston: G. K. Hall, Twayne, 1987.

After a brief survey of *WT*'s reception history, this book provides a scene-by-scene, sometimes line-by-line, analysis of the entire play. Sanders views *WT* as both psychologically realistic and embodying an archetypal pattern of loss and redemption. His discussion of 1.2, for example, teases out hints of pre-existing tensions between Leontes, Polixenes, and Hermione in the scene's dialogue, yet he also comments on the relation between the work's structure and "the paradigm of fairy tale" (30). Sanders argues against interpretation of *WT* in terms of Christian orthodoxy, yet he emphasizes the restorative powers of Time and Nature, as epitomized in Paulina's phrase, "Dear life redeems you" (5.3.103). Throughout the study Sanders comments on poetic style and tone and on the fluidity of the transitions between various movements of the plot, especially the tragic and comic halves of the play.

167. Siemon, James Edward. "'But It Appears She Lives': Iteration in *The Winter's Tale.*" *PMLA* 89 (1974): 10–16. Repr. in Bloom (no. 178).

This article argues that structural repetition in *WT* reinforces the play's emphasis on the loss of goodness through human error and its restoration by the gods. Siemon notes, for example, that Polixenes' accusing Perdita of seducing Florizel parallels Leontes' accusing Hermione of adultery. Siemon emphasizes the mixture of good and evil in human experience; stressing the role of providence (with Camillo and Paulina as its agents), he also assesses the evidence that Hermione actually dies and is restored to life. He notes, for example, that Leontes accepts Paulina's invitation to view Hermione's body (3.2.203–4), and Leontes confirms that he saw her dead (5.3.139–40). He also argues that, according to dramatic convention, the figure who appears in Antigonus's dream (3.3) must be Hermione's ghost.

168. Sokol, B. J. *Art and Illusion in "The Winter's Tale."* Manchester: Manchester Univ. Press, 1994. Distributed in the U. S. by St. Martin's Press.

This study argues that *WT* investigates the moral status of art, rather than univocally celebrating its redemptive power. After an initial survey of "Aesthetic Codes and Renaissance Concepts" (chap. 1, 10–30), Sokol suggests that personal reformation in *WT* derives from art's analysis of the

darker side of human nature. Chap. 2 (31–54) interprets Leontes' irrational jealousy in terms of couvade syndrome, a condition afflicting expec-
tant fathers with a range of physical and psychological symptoms, including excessive fear of marital instability. In chap. 3 (55–84), Sokol argues
that a painted statue would evoke fears of idolatry and excessive sensuality, and yet Paulina's restraint of Leontes in 5.3 enables "true symbolisa-
tion, acknowledging separateness" (79) and thus facilitates the acceptance
of loss and guilt. Chap. 4 (85–115) analyzes the work of the historical
Giulio Romano, with emphasis on its erotic, sometimes threatening qualities,
and chap. 5 (116–41) stresses the anxieties that haunt the Bohemian scenes, in
which Perdita's purity is qualified by her alleged bastardy and by the possibility that she will become Florizel's concubine. Chap. 6 (142–66) compares Camillo and Paulina as creators of illusion. Sokol argues that the
marriage between an essentially worldly Camillo and the spiritual Paulina
suggests that art must "bridge the contemplative versus active divide" (164) if
it is to "instil reality" (163). The concluding chapter (167–82) argues that
Shakespeare's art achieves its vision of the human potential for nobility
only by confronting the dark forces explored throughout the play and
concentrated in Autolycus, whom Sokol sees as the embodiment of indi-
vidualistic libido and of the deception that, paradoxically, is sometimes a
necessary means of doing good.

169. Tayler, Edward William. *Nature and Art in Renaissance Literature.*
New York: Columbia Univ. Press, 1964. Chap. on *WT* repr. in Hunt (no.
179).

Tayler explains (especially 11–37) various Renaissance attitudes toward
the relation between Art and Nature, ranging from the charge that Art
was a counterfeit to the claim that Art reforms the fallen world. His
chapter on *WT* (121–41) argues that the pastoral sheep-shearing scene (4.4)
associates Florizel and Perdita with "innocence and artless Nature" (130)
and suggests an idealized "simple world by which the more complex one
might be judged" (133). Tayler stresses that Shakespeare uses traditional
ideas about Nature and Art as terms of unresolved, witty debate. Yet
Tayler also suggests that the revelation that the statue of Hermione is the
woman herself implies that triumphant human Art is, in the last analysis,
Nature. The chapter provides brief comments on *Cym* and *Tmp*.

F. Stage History; Performance Criticism; Film and Television Versions.

170. Bartholomeusz, Dennis. *"The Winter's Tale" in Performance in England and America, 1611–1976.* Cambridge: Cambridge Univ. Press, 1982.

This book provides an analytical history and evaluation of performances of *WT* (including adaptations), with attention to stage and set design, costuming, music and dance, acting styles, treatments of the text, and trends in interpretation. Bartholomeusz discusses 62 productions, beginning with imaginative re-creation (based on extensive scholarly evidence) of performances in the early seventeenth century. The work has 55 black-and-white illustrations. The author argues that only in performance is the "imagined form" (2) of a play realized, and yet deep understanding of the text is prerequisite for adequate realization of the work's poetic, dramatic, and theatrical values. Less relativistic than some performance critics (cf. Lanier [no. 262]), Bartholomeusz thus finds that 18th-century adaptations such as David Garrick's *Florizel and Perdita* revised Shakespeare's "deliberate disorganisation" in accordance with "a more limited neo-classical ideal of form" (41). He also criticizes Charles Kean's 19th-century version, set in 330 BC, for its emphasis on historical realism through "exact and brilliant spectacle" (82) rather than fidelity to Shakespeare's text. In the twentieth century, Bartholomeusz believes, performances of *WT* by directors such as Harley Granville-Barker began to integrate a respect for English Renaissance stagecraft into modern theatrical practice and thus do justice to the union of disparate forms and the imaginative freedom of the text. Bartholomeusz provides sensitive commentary on the interaction between Shakespeare's text and the vision of strong directors such as Peter Brook and Trevor Nunn.

171. Draper, R. P. *The Winter's Tale.* Text and Performance. General ed. Michael Scott. London: Macmillan, 1985.

This book discusses *WT* through literary and performance criticism. Part 1 (9–44) discusses tragicomic genre and structure, especially the relation between *WT*'s "destructive and creative, tragic and comic halves" (14). Draper analyzes characters and poetic style in the context of a plot development that is linked to images of seasonal change. Part 2 (45–76) discusses *WT*'s performance history, with emphasis on productions directed by Trevor Nunn (Royal Shakespeare Company, 1969); Trevor Nunn and John Barton (Royal Shakespeare Company, 1976); Jane Howell (no. 174);

and Ronald Eyre (Royal Shakespeare Company, 1982). Draper's commentary on sets, costuming, and characterization (especially performances by Ian McKellan, Patrick Stewart, Jeremy Kemp, Sheila Hancock, Judi Dench, and Margaret Tyzack) often centers on efforts to balance realism with a sense of the marvelous.

172. Frey, Charles. *Shakespeare's Vast Romance: A Study of "The Winter's Tale."* Columbia: Univ. of Missouri Press, 1980.

Frey provides a comprehensive treatment of *WT* with an emphasis on "the question of how an informed spectator or reader may appropriately respond to the unfolding play" (47). Chap. 2 (9–48) analyzes records of productions and audience responses from 1611 to 1977, as well as major criticism. Frey concludes that neoclassical and Victorian preconceptions about theater and modern concern for abstract themes have led to diminished attention to how textual meaning is conveyed in performance, a problem partially addressed in productions by Harley Granville-Barker and Peter Brook. Chap. 3 (49–113) interprets *WT* through source study and comparison with previous literary works. Frey argues that *WT*'s alteration of Greene's *Pandosto* provides psychological depth and an affirmation of the regenerative power of time. For Frey, the romances dramatize the restoration of familial and social harmony through the revival of faith in the forces of "natural regeneration" (94) that express the divine and are "mysteriously linked with Art" (60). He explores the manner in which this "religious affirmation ... assumes a beautiful and convincing variety of kaleidoscopic forms" (91). Chap. 4 (114–69) offers a close reading of the language, characterization, plot structure, and visual spectacle of *WT* as the play unfolds in performance. Frey discusses, for example, the ironic contrast between the language of harmony and the threat of discord in the first two scenes; the parallels between scenes in the tragic and comic portions of the play; and the centrality of the multifaceted concept of "faith": interpersonal trust, "belief in providence, fidelity to vows of love, sincerity, uncritical confidence" in humanity and the natural order (161).

173. Granville-Barker, Harley. Preface to *The Winter's Tale.* 1912. Repr. in *More Prefaces to Shakespeare*, ed. Edward M. Moore, 19–25. Princeton: Princeton Univ. Press, 1974. Repr. in Hunt (no. 179).

Granville-Barker admires the successful artifice of *WT*, including the use of Time as transitional chorus; the formal contrasts among prose, humor, poetry, and music in the statue scene (5.3); and the symmetry of having Paulina marry Camillo. He contrasts Leontes' jealousy with Othello's, the former more "perverse, ignoble, pitiable" (21). Granville-Barker also argues that *WT*'s mixture of comedy and tragedy helps to sustain the audience's interest; he suggests, for example, that a touch of the ridiculous in Leontes' character renders him human and therefore sympathetic. Moore's introduction to *More Prefaces* (8–18) discusses Granville-Barker's contribution to Shakespearean production, notably his use of formal sets rather than elaborate scenery and his emphasis on dramatic poetry as an expression of the inner reality of the characters.

174. Howell, Jane, director; Jonathan Miller, producer. *The Winter's Tale.* The BBC "Shakespeare Plays" Series, 1980.

This television version makes only a few cuts in Shakespeare's text. Howell uses spare, stylized scenery and appears to have encouraged a somewhat restrained style of performance. The cast includes Jeremy Kemp (Leontes), Anna Calder-Marshall (Hermione), Margaret Tyzack (Paulina), David Burke (Camillo), and Rikki Fulton (Autolycus). Reviewers have sometimes praised this production's elegant, expressionistic style; alternatively, they have lamented its timidity. The videotape is available from The Writing Company and elsewhere. For further information and commentary, see Rothwell and Melzer (no. 24), item 673.

175. McCabe, Richard. "Autolycus in *The Winter's Tale.*" *Players of Shakespeare 4: Further Essays in Shakespearean Performance by Players with the Royal Shakespeare Company,* ed. Robert Smallwood, 60–70. Cambridge: Cambridge Univ. Press, 1998.

McCabe describes his development of the role of Autolycus, which he performed in two Royal Shakespeare Company productions (1992 and 1993). He stresses the complexity of Autolycus's character, mentioning his fear of "beating and hanging" (4.3.29) as well as his arrogance. McCabe discusses several reasons why audiences find Autolycus appealing despite his selfishness and amorality: we feel liberated by his vitality; we admire those who "dare to challenge our comfortable certainties" (68); and we forgive him because we recognize a bit of him in ourselves. McCabe concludes that our forgiveness of Autolycus prepares us to pardon the repentant Leontes in *WT*'s final act.

176. Murray, Peter B. *Shakespeare's Imagined Persons: The Psychology of Role-Playing and Acting.* Lanham, Md.: Barnes and Noble; London: Macmillan, 1996.

This book argues that proto-behaviorist psychology (including that of Aristotle and Montaigne) influenced Shakespeare's understanding of the significance of role-playing in the construction of human identity. The chapter on *WT* (173–78) discusses the manner in which Perdita's absorption in the roles of daughter, loving maiden, hostess, and the goddess Flora enable her to attain "a fullness of being in imaginative action" (177). Her performance, Murray concludes, embodies Shakespeare's vision of the power of dramatic art to express human potential.

See also nos. 141, 142, 143, 157, 160, 163, 165, 179, 180.

G. Reception History; Adaptations; The Winter's Tale as Source for and Influence on Later Writers and Works.

See nos. 140, 166, 170, 172, 179.

H. Pedagogy.

177. Young, Bruce W. "Teaching the Unrealistic Realism of *The Winter's Tale.*" In Hunt (no. 95), 87–93.

Acknowledging that many students deplore *WT*'s apparent lack of realism, Young recommends encouraging them to ask whether their own lives are, in fact, less incredible than Shakespeare's fiction. Through class brainstorming (often in writing), Young initiates discussions on the difficulty of believing in the possibility of human love and on the challenges of religious faith. Young concludes that *WT* "challenges our notion of what is possible" and, in doing so, helps us see that our own narrowness of vision "is as responsible as anything for the misery, the destructive conflicts, that enter our lives" (93).

I. Collections.

178. Bloom, Harold, ed. *William Shakespeare's "The Winter's Tale."* Modern Critical Interpretations. New York: Chelsea House, 1987.

This anthology reprints Barton (no. 43), Frey (in no. 102), Knights (no. 159), Neely (no. 161), Siemon (no. 167), and an excerpt from Knight, *The Crown of Life* (no. 71). Louis Martz (123–38) argues that *WT* progresses through three stages: the first embodies the ethos of Greek tragedy, the second a realm of timeless pagan pastoral, the third the world of Renaissance Christian humanism. Richard Studing (139–49) describes the Bohemian scenes as corrupted, rather than idealized, pastoral. Bloom's introduction (1–5) affirms *WT*'s use of wonder to move us beyond nihilism. Bloom includes a bibliography (155–57) and index (161–65), but he eliminates the original authors' bibliographical notes.

179. Hunt, Maurice, ed. *"The Winter's Tale": Critical Essays*. Garland Reference Library of the Humanities, vol. 1846. Shakespeare Criticism, vol. 14. New York: Garland, 1995.

This book reprints literary criticism and theater reviews from 1802 to 1995, including the following items annotated elsewhere in this volume: Gourlay (no. 151), McDonald (no. 152), Hartwig's essay on *WT* as tragicomedy revised in no. 65, a version of Hunt's discussion of labor in *WT* (see no. 67), and extracts from Felperin (no. 58), R. G. Hunter (no. 68), Tayler (no. 169), and Granville-Barker (no. 173). The remaining critical essays are William Hazlitt's commentary (65–71) on *WT*'s major characters; Samuel Taylor Coleridge's notes (72–75) on Leontes' jealousy and on poetic style; Arthur Quiller-Couch's criticism (82–93) of the play's workmanship; F. David Hoeniger's article (94–105) on the centrality of art, nature, and rebirth in *WT*; Northrop Frye's discussion (106–18) of emblematic recognition scenes and the redemptive power of nature; Inga-Stina Ewbank's essay (139–55) on the destructive yet revelatory powers of Time; Peter Lindenbaum's commentary (200–219) on *WT*'s affirmation of healthy sexual love and the play's versions of pastoral; Carol Thomas Neely's analysis (243–56) of the power of differing styles of speech to corrupt or to renew human life; Richard Proudfoot's discussion (280–97) of the play's two-part structure; and Kay Stockholder's psychoanalytical study (319–34) of family relations and sexual passion in the play. In an original essay (361–79), David Bergeron argues for the pervasive influence of Apollo in *WT*. Hunt's introductory discussion of "The Critical Legacy" (3–56) provides valuable analysis of the play's reception and performance history.

180. Muir, Kenneth, ed. *Shakespeare, "The Winter's Tale": A Casebook*. London: Macmillan, 1968. Nashville: Aurora Press, 1970. Repr. often.

Part 1 of this collection (23–66) includes 46 brief comments from playgoers, poets and dramatists, and critics, from 1611 to 1951, including Simon Forman, Ben Jonson, Samuel Johnson, William Hazlitt, S. T. Coleridge, Lytton Strachey, Ellen Terry, Harold Goddard, and Arthur Sewall. Part 2 (69–233) includes the following items annotated elsewhere in this volume: Coghill (no. 157) and excerpts from Knight (no. 71), Stauffer (no.

83), Tillyard (no. 84), Traversi (no. 85), and Bethell (no. 155). Additional items include Inga-Stina Ewbank's essay (98–115) on the destructive yet revelatory powers of time; Ernest Schanzer's analysis (87–97) of parallels and contrasts between the first and second halves of *WT*; Harold S. Wilson's discussion (151–58) of nature and art in the context of possible sources such as George Puttenham's *Arte of English Poesie*; Northrop Frye's discussion (184–97) of "the redeeming and reviving power of a nature identified with art, grace, and love" (197) and adumbrated in the play's recognition scenes (especially 5.3); M. M. Mahood's analysis (214–31) of the multiple meanings of key terms such as "play," "nature," and "grace"; and Louis MacNeice's poem (232–33) "Autolycus." Muir's introduction (11–20) surveys the work's reception history and emphasizes the growing awareness of *WT*'s artistic complexity.

J. Bibliographies.

See nos. 95, 110, 111, 112, 113, 140, 141, 143, 163, 179.

V. THE TEMPEST

A. Editions.

181. Furness, Horace Howard, ed. *The Tempest.* A New Variorum Edition of Shakespeare. Philadelphia: Lippincott, 1892. Repr. New York: American Scholar Publications, 1966.

In his preface (v–xi), Furness discusses characterization, especially the complexity of Caliban; William Davenant and John Dryden's adaptation; and the theory that Jacob Ayrer's *The Fair Sidea* is a major source. The text is based on the First Folio. Textual notes and extensive commentary from 18th- and 19th-century scholars and critics appear on each page. The appendix (271–457) surveys scholarship on the text; date; possible sources (some of them reprinted); and a range of critical issues. Settings for two songs that may have been used by Shakespeare's company are reprinted. The appendix also includes excerpts of criticism (chiefly on characterization) by S. Johnson, W. Hazlitt, S. T. Coleridge, Edward Dowden, A. W. Schlegel, and many others. Furness reprints the 1674 operatic version of *Tmp*, based on the Dryden-Davenant adaptation. (See nos. 260 and 266 on Furness's erroneous identification of the 1674 adaptation by Thomas Shadwell with the 1670 Dryden-Davenant text.) The "Plan of the Work" (451–57) includes a partial list of works cited. The volume concludes with an index (459–65), and the 1966 reprint includes (I–XXIII) Louis Marder's *The Tempest: A Supplementary Bibliography* (1892–1965).

182. Kermode, Frank, ed. *The Tempest.* 6th ed. The Arden Shakespeare, second series. Cambridge: Harvard Univ. Press, 1958. Repr. often. Distributed by Thomas Nelson and Sons.

Kermode's introduction (xi–xciii) discusses the date and text (based on the First Folio); sources, including the relation of *Tmp* to travel literature and the discovery of the New World (with emphasis on the concept of the providential voyage); the traditions of pastoral, tragicomedy, masque, and romance; and the themes of the play, notably the relation of art and nature. Caliban, Kermode argues, represents nature devoid of grace or art. The evil sorcery of Sycorax is natural magic, he believes, whereas Prospero's supernatural magic is "the means of Grace" (xlviii) and is capable of reforming nature. Prospero's art also represents, for Kermode, the civilizing power of education and culture; yet art is efficacious only on those characters of inherent nobility who choose to cooperate with a harmonious world order whose laws are revealed by the romance genre. Kermode adds a brief survey of criticism through 1948 and a note defending the view that the Folio text is based on a transcript by Ralph Crane. Textual notes and extensive commentary appear at the bottom of each page. Appendices (135–71) provide additional commentary (especially on Ariel); extracts from sources (Strachey's *True Reportory of the Wracke and Redemption of Sir Thomas Gates*, Jourdain's *Discovery of the Bermudas*, Montaigne's "Of the Cannibals," and Ovid's *Metamorphoses*); comments on early staging; and three pieces of music that may have been used by Shakespeare's company. Kermode's introduction is among the most influential interpretations of this play. See also nos. 187, 199, 205, 222b. Excerpts are reprinted in nos. 270, 274, 275.

183. Langbaum, Robert, ed. *The Tempest.* Signet Classic Shakespeare. Newly revised edition. New York: Penguin Putnam, 1998.

Langbaum's introduction (lxiii-lxxvii) suggests that *Tmp* is the culmination of Shakespeare's art, especially in its paradoxical, tragicomic affirmation that "the evil, the violence, the tragedy are all part of a providential design" (lxiv). Characters who possess a capacity for wonder, Langbaum argues, can see order behind apparent disorder. He emphasizes the importance of Renaissance conceptions of degree in our interpretation of the characters and their responsibilities, and he offers an ambivalent response to new historicist approaches. The text, based on the First Folio, is followed (89–90) by a textual note and a list of emendations. Annotation appears at the bottom of each page. Langbaum argues that there is no source for *Tmp*'s plot, but "there are documents that are relevant to it" (91). He reprints (93–105) excerpts from travel literature, Montaigne's "Of the Cannibals," and Ovid's *Metamorphoses*. Langbaum also reprints (106–55) criticism by Samuel Taylor Coleridge, Tillyard (excerpt from no. 84), Greenblatt (excerpt from no. 197), Knox (no. 203), Leininger (no. 204). The volume concludes with a brief stage history by Sylvan Barnet (180–90) and a selected bibliography (191–205). For annotation of the contributions of the general editor, see no. 5.

184. Orgel, Stephen, ed. *The Tempest.* The Oxford Shakespeare. Oxford: Oxford Univ. Press, 1987.

In his introduction (1–87), Orgel argues that *Tmp* is a self-contradictory text that stimulates a range of disparate readings and performances. He notes that *Tmp* shares with the court masque a celebration of royal

power, especially its magical ability to resolve social and moral discords
into harmony; yet Shakespeare presents Prospero as a seriously flawed
ruler, and the interruption of the wedding masque by Prospero's remem-
brance of Caliban's plot reminds us not only of the world's intractable
evils, but also of Prospero's infirmities. *Tmp*'s ending, Orgel concludes,
includes hints of future conflict as well as Prospero's claim that he seeks
reconciliation. Orgel's discussion of the text and date (56–64) includes
evaluation of major scholarship on the First Folio. The illustrated stage
history (64–87) discusses the spectacular Dryden-Davenant adaptation and
the Shadwell operatic version; the influence on performances of Darwinism and the issue of colonialism; and the 20th-century release of the play's
darker passions in productions by Peter Brook and others. Textual notes
and commentary appear at the bottom of each page. Appendices (209–43)
provide additional textual notes on lineation; reprint excerpts of sources;
and discuss Shakespeare's knowledge of seamanship and his use of music.
Orgel includes two settings for songs believed to be used by Shakespeare's
company. The introduction, commentary, and appendices are indexed
(245–48). See also nos. 209, 237, and 238 by Orgel. For commentary, see
Cox (no. 222b) and Pierce (no. 238a).

**185. Righter, Anne [Anne Barton], ed. *The Tempest.* The New Penguin
Shakespeare. Harmondsworth, England: Penguin Books, 1968. Repr.
often.**

Righter's introduction (7–51) emphasizes *Tmp*'s mystery and ambiguity. She analyzes the ways in which the play evokes wonder and undermines our confidence that we can distinguish between illusion and reality.
Uncertainty with regard to Prospero's motives contributes to the play's
aura of mystery, she argues, and the audience is made aware of the
subjectivity and relativity of characters' interpretations of events. The
masque and the "revels" speech (4.1) and the epilogue, she argues, are the
culmination of *Tmp*'s dramatization of a dreamlike experience that
ultimately applies not only to the play but also to the audience's experience of the world outside the theater. Appendices provide commentary
notes; a brief discussion of the First Folio text and a list of editorial
emendations; and settings for "Full Fathom Five" and "Where the Bee
Sucks" attributed to Robert Johnson and possibly used in performances
during Shakespeare's lifetime.

**185a. Vaughan, Virginia Mason, and Alden T. Vaughan, eds. *The
Tempest.* The Arden Shakespeare, third series. Walton-on-Thames, U.K.:
Thomas Nelson and Sons, 1999.**

The Vaughans' introduction (1–138) emphasizes *Tmp*'s "elusiveness"

(17) and its ability to evoke a sense of wonder. The editors discuss approaches to the play's genre (tragicomedy or romance); structure; music (with reprints of Robert Johnson's settings of two songs); and versification. They then discuss characters, underscoring the ambiguity of Prospero's motives; touches of complexity in Miranda and others; and the multiple interpretations of Caliban. The section on historical contexts and sources assesses the evidence for the play's relation to travel literature (including William Strachey's *True Reportory of the Wracke and Redemption of Sir Thomas Gates* and Sylvester Jourdain's *Discovery of the Bermudas*) and the ideology of colonialism; the Vaughans see African and Irish contexts as at least as relevant as American. The editors next consider the possible influence of medieval romances; classical works such as Virgil's *Aeneid* and Ovid's *Metamorphoses*; and debates concerning "civility" and "barbarism," especially Montaigne's "Of the Caniballes." They discuss the sources and nature of Prospero's magic and the influence of the court masque. The section on the play's performance and reception history argues that *Tmp*'s "'second-world' structure" (74) and its dramatization of basic human relationships are the grounds of its extensive influence and adaptability. The Vaughans discuss major stage performances and film versions of the play; adaptations and appropriations, including the Dryden-Davenant *Tmp*, Thomas Shadwell's opera, Percy Mackaye's *Caliban by the Yellow Sands*, Peter Greenaway's *Prospero's Books*, and others; and four centuries of critical commentary, including the interpretations of Samuel Taylor Coleridge, Anna Jameson, Edward Dowden, Octave Mannoni, Leslie Fiedler, and others. Their discussion of the text accepts the theory that the First Folio version was probably set from a transcript by Ralph Crane, who may have added act and scene divisions and stage directions. Spelling is modernized; extensive textual and commentary notes appear at the bottom of each page. Appendices reprint extracts from Strachey; Montaigne; Browning, "Caliban upon Setebos"; José Enrique Rodó, *Ariel*; and Mannoni. The introduction and commentary are indexed. The volume includes 22 illustrations.

See also no. 271a.

B. Dating and Textual Studies.

186. Wells, Stanley, and Gary Taylor, with John Jowett and William Montgomery. *William Shakespeare: A Textual Companion.* Oxford: Clarendon Press, 1987.
   This book is a companion to *William Shakespeare: The Complete Works* (Oxford: Clarendon Press, 1986; see no. 3). The authors' discussion

of *Tmp* in "Canon and Chronology of Shakespeare's Plays" (132) argues for a date of 1611. The later section (612–17) provides detailed textual commentary and argues that the Folio text is based on a transcript by Ralph Crane, who probably elaborated the stage directions.

See also nos. 40, 52, 181, 182, 183, 184, 185, 185a, 222a, 238, 274.

C. Influences; Sources; Intertextuality; Historical and Intellectual Contexts; Topicality.

187. Barker, Francis, and Peter Hulme. "'Nymphs and Reapers Heavily Vanish': The Discursive Con-Texts of *The Tempest*." In *Alternative Shakespeares*, ed. John Drakakis, 191–205. London: Methuen, 1985. Repr. in Graff and Phelan (no. 271a) and White (no. 277a).

Barker and Hulme position *Tmp* within the discourse of English colonialism. Grounding their work on a study of continuities between the play and "congruent texts" (196) that express colonialist assumptions, the authors maintain that *Tmp* reflects the ideological conflicts of English Renaissance culture. They argue, for example, that the subjugation of Caliban for attempting to rape Miranda parallels the enslavement of native populations in the New World on the grounds of their "treacherous" nature. Yet they also emphasize aspects of the play that reveal the text's anxiety with regard to the political assumptions that rationalize Prospero's authority: they note, for example, the magician's insecurity and excessive wrath when he recalls (4.1) Caliban's plot against his life. An influential instance of cultural materialism, this essay provides a lucid introduction to recent discourse theory. Hulme expands this interpretation in chap. 3 of *Colonial Encounters: Europe and the Native Caribbean, 1492–1797* (London: Methuen, 1986), 89–134. Among the commentaries on this article and on Hulme's book are nos. 191, 193, 202, 220, 222b, 238a, 239, and 242.

188. Berger, Karol. "Prospero's Art." *Shakespeare Studies* 10 (1977): 211–39.

This article argues that Prospero's art is based upon Neoplatonic magic as described by Florentine Neoplatonist Marsilio Ficino and disseminated through such works as Cornelius Agrippa's *De occulta philosophia*. Berger emphasizes that Prospero's art works through music and theatrical spectacle, and that its aim is to teach "the wisdom of pardon, sacrifice, and reconciliation" (236) through effects on the imagination. For Berger, *Tmp* suggests that the wisdom embodied in works of art can transform the real world only if the audience freely participates in the artist's vision; Prospero's renunciation of magic and his appeal to the audience in the epilogue are thus necessary steps toward the goal of personal and social transformation.

189. Bevington, David. "*The Tempest* and the Jacobean Court Masque." In *The Politics of the Stuart Court Masque*, ed. David Bevington and Peter Holbrook, 218–43. Cambridge: Cambridge Univ. Press, 1998.

This essay argues that the masque in *Tmp* is designed to enable the audience of the public theaters to experience a courtly spectacle similar to that provided for the royalty and aristocracy. Bevington suggests that *Tmp* may have been written with the betrothal of Princess Elizabeth and the Elector Palatine in mind, and that there are parallels between Prospero and James I, both of whom are somewhat self-indulgent intellectuals, "visionary about peace" (221) and predominantly benevolent yet sometimes neglectful of their duties. Contrasting *Tmp* with Thomas Campion's *The Lords' Masque*, a work that focuses upon celebration of monarchy, Bevington concludes that the ultimate authority in *Tmp* is the artist, and that the primary patron is the public, to whom Prospero appeals for applause (and, implicitly, future support) in the epilogue.

190. Brown, Paul. "'This Thing of Darkness I Acknowledge Mine': *The Tempest* and the Discourse of Colonialism." In *Political Shakespeare: New Essays in Cultural Materialism*, ed. Jonathan Dollimore and Alan Sinfield, 48–71. Ithaca: Cornell Univ. Press, 1985. Repr. in nos. 271 and 271a.

Brown affirms the participation of *Tmp* in colonialist discourse. He argues, for example, that the play produces in Caliban an image of a savage alien that must be subjugated and civilized. Yet Brown stresses that the construction of the alien as a threat necessarily confers upon the Other a dangerous power to challenge authority: Caliban becomes "a linguistic subject of the master language" (61), yet he voices his resistance to Prospero's hegemony by uttering curses. Adopting strategies that are influential in new historicist criticism, the essay explores numerous additional ways in which *Tmp* embodies a radical political ambivalence, both affirming and disrupting colonialist ideology. For commentary, see nos. 226 and 271a.

191. Cheyfitz, Eric. *The Poetics of Imperialism: Translation and Colonization from "The Tempest" to "Tarzan."* New York: Oxford Univ. Press, 1991.

Interpretation of *Tmp* is woven throughout this book's argument concerning the poetics of imperialism. Cheyfitz argues that Prospero represents European colonizers who rationalize conquest by casting themselves as civilizers of barbarians; the imperialist turns to violence when the "savage" is interpreted as "treacherous." For Cheyfitz, this imperialist fantasy entails

repressing one's awareness of the challenges of cross-cultural communication, and, consequently, of the difficulties of translation as genuine
dialogue; the colonizer practices a specious "translation" that projects the
assumptions of the conqueror upon the colonized subject, thus creating a
"fiction of understanding" (82). *Tmp*, he believes, affirms the Renaissance
imperialist fantasy of the power of rhetoric to subdue the world as
though by magic. Although Prospero despairs of this project momentarily
in the "Revels" speech (4.1.146–63), all imperialists, including Prospero,
Cheyfitz claims, "continually [resublimate] their despair in hallucinations
of immediate power" (141). Drawing upon Hulme (see no. 187), Cheyfitz
insists that the play cannot transcend topical and political concerns; like
other imperialist documents, it is "obsessed with putting people in what
the ruling class understands as their proper places" (86). Cheyfitz thus
questions the entire concept of "great art" (87). He also disagrees with
Greenblatt's argument (no. 196) that *Tmp* brings the audience toward a
more complete perception of Caliban's otherness than Prospero attains.
Throughout this study, Cheyfitz seeks to undermine the assumption of
the superiority of Western democracy and capitalism that he sees as still
influential in American foreign policy.

192. Curry, Walter Clyde. "Sacerdotal Science in Shakespeare's *The Tempest.*" Chap. 6 of *Shakespeare's Philosophical Patterns*, 163–99. 2nd edition.
Baton Rouge: Louisiana State Univ. Press, 1959. Repr. Gloucester, Mass.:
Peter Smith, 1968.

This study argues that Prospero's magic is pagan "sacerdotal science"
or theurgy, defined as the ability to "energize in the gods or to control
other beneficent spiritual intelligences in the working of miraculous
effects" (167). Curry argues that *Tmp* is based on the Neoplatonism of
Plotinus, Porphyry, and Iamblichus, made available to Shakespeare
through Ficino's translations and Latin works by Cicero. This philosophy, Curry believes, provides the basis for a clear distinction between
Prospero's benevolent theurgy and the evil magic of Sycorax, and Curry
stresses that the ultimate goal of theurgy is the union of the practitioner's
soul with the gods. Prospero abjures his magic because, having completed
the work of righting earthly wrongs and cleansing his soul from passions,
he aspires (notably in the epilogue) to the status of an impassive divinity.
Although readers should update Curry's work by reference to such
studies as nos. 188, 207, 208, 215, and 240, his book provides a clear
introduction to the Neoplatonism that often has been regarded as fundamental to an understanding of this play.

193. Felperin, Howard. "The Tempest in Our Time." In Felperin (no.
101), 170–90.

This essay argues that political readings of *Tmp* are not demystifications of the play; instead, they are allegories produced by a transaction between the text and cultural presuppositions that differ from those that contribute to religious or biographical allegories. Felperin discusses the critical history of *Tmp* in relation to the political processes that influence canon formation. He evaluates the political efficacy of cultural materialism and new historicism, concluding that an evolving canon can be a battleground on which political criticism of greater power than developed to date may thrive. See also nos. 223, 224.

194. Fiedler, Leslie A. *The Stranger in Shakespeare.* New York: Stein and Day, 1972; London: Croon Helm, 1973.

This book argues that Joan of Arc, Shylock, Othello, and Caliban represent the archetypal stranger who evokes both wonder and fear and who raises questions concerning the boundaries of the human in the foundational myths of Western culture. The chapter on *Tmp* (199–253) discusses Caliban as compound of American Indian, African, and witch. Fiedler relates the character to numerous sources—including *The Aeneid*, Ovidian poetry, Montaigne's "Of the Cannibals," and Renaissance travel literature—in which European civilization confronts the Alien. He stresses the violence and lust in Shakespeare's characterization of Caliban, yet he also notes the character's capacity for poetic wonder. Fiedler emphasizes that *Tmp* struggles toward recognition of Caliban's humanity and thus toward acknowledgment of forces within the European Prospero's personality that have been repressed.

195. Gillies, John. *Shakespeare and the Geography of Difference.* Cambridge: Cambridge Univ. Press, 1994. Extract repr. in White (no. 277a).

This book's introduction (1–39) discusses "Shakespeare's construction of 'Europe'" (2) and of exotic lands that lie beyond it; it also examines the politics governing actual and imaginary relations among Europeans and inhabitants of mysterious or quasi-mythological locations and cultures. Gillies stresses Shakespeare's use of "a rich geographic tradition that is already moralised," especially in its treatment of "human difference" (4). He argues (especially 40–45) that *Tmp*'s treatment of otherness must be understood in the context of the ethnography and "poetic geography" revealed throughout Shakespeare's canon. A subsequent section (140–55) analyzes the "natural and moral history" (141) of Prospero's island in terms of three recurrent myths: (1) the "dispersal myth" that identifies Caliban as an outcast from humankind; (2) the "plantation myth" in which Prospero and Miranda attempt to reclaim the island and civilize it; and (3) the "'renewal' or 'regeneration' myth" (141) in which we experience visions of redemption, such as the wedding masque in 4.1. Gillies concludes that, although Shakespeare does not grant Caliban the element of dignity that he confers upon other aliens such as Othello or Shylock, he nonetheless casts an ironic light upon the play's utopian elements, thus creating a "blend of reaction and subversion" (153) in his treatment of the myths that rationalize colonialism.

196. Greenblatt, Stephen. "Learning to Curse: Aspects of Linguistic Colonialism in the Sixteenth Century." In *First Images of America*, ed. Fredi Chiapelli, 561-80. Berkeley and Los Angeles: Univ. of California Press, 1976. Repr. in Greenblatt's *Learning to Curse: Essays in Early Modern Culture*, 16-39. New York: Routledge, 1990. Excerpt repr. in Bloom (no. 271).

Greenblatt's new historicist analysis affirms *Tmp*'s ambivalence concerning Prospero's attempts to civilize Caliban (who may be analogous to a colonial subject) by teaching him language. For Greenblatt, the conflict between the play's affirmation of European superiority and its acknowledgment that Caliban represents an ineradicable destructive element within human nature—and thus within Prospero—is unresolved. For commentary, see nos. 191, 235, and 238a.

197. Greenblatt, Stephen. "Martial Law in the Land of Cockaigne." In *Shakespearean Negotiations: The Circulation of Social Energy in Renaissance England*, 129-63. Berkeley and Los Angeles: Univ. of California Press, 1988. Repr. in Ryan (no. 106b). Extract repr. in White (no. 277a) and Langbaum (no. 183).

This chapter discusses the theatrical/social practice of producing anxiety in order to shape identity and promote obedience. In *Tmp*, the essay argues, Prospero's art produces anxiety and relieves it primarily by enacting pardon (an act that confirms Prospero's power). Greenblatt compares the play with William Strachey's account (see Kermode [no. 182]) of the imposition of martial law upon potential colonists as a means of forcing them to proceed to Virginia after their shipwreck on an island that provided opportunities for subversion of authority. For Greenblatt, *Tmp* differs from Strachey's pamphlet in its ambivalence: the play sometimes subverts Prospero's authority, not least by focusing upon the ruler's confession of limitations and by the epilogue's circulating to the audience the authority to grant pardon.

198. Hamilton, Donna B. *Virgil and "The Tempest": The Politics of Imitation.* Columbus: Ohio State Univ. Press, 1990.

Hamilton argues that *Tmp* participates in the debates over royal absolutism versus constitutionalism that were especially intense in 1610. *The Aeneid*, she believes, is the appropriate work for Shakespeare to imitate in this context because of the epic's political significance: Virgil not only praises Caesar Augustus but also evaluates his actions. Similarly, she argues, Shakespeare praises James I and echoes his claim that the king is godlike, yet he also gives voice to fears that subjects will become slaves. Furthermore, she sees *The Aeneid* as the archetypal treatment of colonialism, an issue she discusses in the context of debates concerning royal prerogative and the rights of subjects. Part 1 (11–66) discusses the Renaissance theory of imitation as the creation of a new work that transmutes elements of the old. Hamilton argues that Shakespeare combines political themes with the allegorical tradition that treats Aeneas's journey as a progress through trial toward wisdom. Part 2 (67–104) discusses Shakespeare's use of Virgilian materials in visionary scenes that teach the rewards of self-restraint and the punishments of excessive ambition; the relationship between Ferdinand and Miranda is founded on a reciprocity that is analogous to constitutional monarchy, in which power is shared. Part 3 (105–32) argues that dialogue among Prospero, Ariel, and Caliban expresses divergent views of the power relations between James I and his subjects. Hamilton concludes that Prospero's renunciation of magic implies that the monarch should accept limited, constitutional power. The epilogue (133–37) affirms that Shakespeare ends the play with a Virgilian form of humility. See also Tudeau-Clayton (no. 213).

199. Hamlin, William H. "Men of Inde: Renaissance Ethnography and *The Tempest.*" *Shakespeare Studies* 22 (1994): 15–44.

Hamlin argues that while some Renaissance ethnographers responded to inhabitants of the New World in ways that served colonialist ideology, others acknowledged differences without subordinating or demonizing the alien. *Tmp*'s portrayal of Caliban, he believes, is ambivalent, yet it moves toward acceptance of Caliban as fully human: the play as a whole refutes Prospero's claim that Caliban is "a born devil on whose nature / Nurture can never stick" (4.1.188–89). This essay draws upon a wealth of primary sources, and it provides a useful critical survey of methods of source study and theories of intertextuality, including commentary on nos. 182, 187, 194, 196.

200. Kastan, David. " 'The Duke of Milan and His Brave Son': Old Histories and New in *The Tempest.*" In *Shakespeare After Theory*, 183–97. New York: Routledge, 1999. Repr. in Graff and Phelan (no. 271a). An earlier version appears in Vaughan and Vaughan (no. 276).

Although he does not deny that *Tmp* participates to some degree in the early modern discourse of colonialism, Kastan argues that the play is more focused upon "European dynastic concerns than European colonial activities" (188). The essay demonstrates the preoccupation of the major characters with the attainment and retention of dynastic power over Naples and Milan. Kastan also links the marriage of Ferdinand and Miranda with that of Princess Elizabeth and Frederick, the Elector Palatine, and with James I's "fantasy of European peace and coherence" (189). He concludes by conceding that the contexts through which we interpret a text are "virtually infinite" and may be "ethical, psychological, theological [or] ... aesthetic," yet he believes that if we wish to "reinsert the play into its own historical moment ... we should look more closely at the old world than the new" (196). Cf. Wilson (no. 216).

201. Kernan, Alvin. *Shakespeare, The King's Playwright: Theater in the Stuart Court, 1603–1613.* New Haven: Yale Univ. Press, 1995.

This book argues that as patronage artist Shakespeare was neither a mere propagandist nor a subversive, but rather an astute commentator on issues of concern to King James I. Chap. 8 (150–68) argues that *Tmp* provides not merely a flattering image of "the patriarchal ruler of the island" (158) but an analysis of European perspectives upon the New World, ranging from Gonzalo's utopianism to the rapacity of Stephano and Trinculo. Kernan also suggests that Shakespeare's vision of his art includes both an affirmation of its moral power and an awareness of its ephemeral nature. He concludes that *Tmp* also reflects the transitory nature of "the great globe itself and all that is in it" (168).

201a. Kirkpatrick, Robin. "The Italy of *The Tempest.*" In Hulme and Sherman (no. 271b), 78–96.

This essay analyzes the conflict in *Tmp* between two Italian influences that Kirkpatrick sees as central to Shakespeare's work: the cynical Realpolitik of Machiavelli and the pastoral idealism of Guarini. For Kirkpatrick, idealism is most concentrated in Miranda, who both evokes and expresses the wonder which "identifies and illuminates the particularities of human value" (91); Prospero's rejoinder to Miranda's admiration of the "brave new world / That has such people in't" (5.1.182–83) expresses a note of disillusionment. The audience, Kirkpatrick concludes, views Prospero from both of these perspectives, seeing him in part as idealistic artist/magician and reformer and in part as Machiavellian schemer. Kirkpatrick also comments on noise/confusion versus music/order as a reflection of the play's two contrasting perspectives.

202. Kirsch, Arthur. "Virtue, Vice, and Compassion in Montaigne and *The Tempest.*" *Studies in English Literature, 1500–1900* 37 (1997): 337–52.

This article argues that Prospero's struggle to overcome impatience and the desire for vengeance illustrates the concept of virtue explicated in Montaigne's "Of Cruelty," an essay that influenced *Tmp*. Both Montaigne and Shakespeare stress that virtue (as opposed to innocence) entails difficult striving against vice: "Many, if not most, of the traits and actions that in recent years have been thought to falsify Prospero's ostensible motives and to signify his intractably tyrannical, if not colonialist, mentality" Kirsch concludes, "are ultimately signs of the struggle of virtue" (342–43). The essay also discusses the role of sympathetic imagination—and thus the potentially beneficent influence of theater—in the generation of compassion.

203. Knox, Bernard. "*The Tempest* and the Ancient Comic Tradition." In *English Stage Comedy*, ed. W. K. Wimsatt, Jr., 52–73. English Institute Essays, 1954. New York: Columbia Univ. Press, 1955. Repr. New York: AMS Press, 1964. Essay repr. in Langbaum (no. 183).

Knox analyzes aspects of *Tmp*'s plot and characterization in relation to conventional depictions of master-slave relationships in ancient Roman comedy. He compares Caliban, Stephano, and Trinculo to the "stupid slaves" of classical comedy who are mocked for their outlandish ambitions and are "suitably punished" and "restored to their proper place and function" (72); Ariel, in contrast, is a "slave whose nature is free," and is "balanced by Ferdinand, the free man and prince, who is enslaved" (66). Knox compares Prospero to the "Plautine old man ... who may in the end turn out to have a heart of gold" (64–65) but who initially displays a foolish irascibility. Knox believes that *Tmp* attains plausibility by balancing its fantastic setting with adherence to established conventions of characterization and structure.

204. Leininger, Lorie Jerrell. "The Miranda Trap: Sexism and Racism in Shakespeare's *Tempest.*" In *The Woman's Part: Feminist Criticism of Shakespeare*, ed. Carolyn R. S. Lenz, Gayle Green, and Carol T. Neely, 285–94. Urbana: Univ. of Illinois Press, 1980. Repr. in Langbaum (no. 183).

Leininger argues that *Tmp* affirms patriarchal and hierarchical values that rationalize the oppression of women and allegedly inferior classes and races. The play utilizes, she believes, an allegorical mode that sees rulers as embodiments of godlike virtues and the working classes and aliens as embodiments of bestial vices. The play thus participates, in her view, in an ideology that rationalizes slavery and conquest. For commentary, see Pierce (no. 238a).

205. Loomba, Ania. *Gender, Race, Renaissance Drama.* Cultural Politics Series. Manchester: Manchester Univ. Press, 1989. Distributed in the United States and Canada by St. Martin's Press. Chap. on *Tmp* repr. in nos. 271a and 277a.

Loomba studies the "confrontation between independent or disorderly women and public and private authority" (1) in English Renaissance drama from the perspective of a feminist scholar in postcolonial India. Responding to the work of Barker and Hulme (no. 187), Brown (no. 190), and Cartelli (see no. 255), Loomba's chapter on *Tmp* (142–58) argues that the struggle for meaning and political value in the play's reception history is related to the polyphony of the text itself. In part, she finds, the play defends colonialism and patriarchy through stereotypical images of women (the white, chaste, and obedient Miranda versus the black, lusty, and rebellious Sycorax) and blacks (Caliban as black rapist). Yet analysis of the relation between Prospero and Caliban, Loomba believes, also reveals the complexity of both the colonizer and the colonial subject, as the subordinate seeks not justice but mastery. This relation, Loomba concludes, parallels the process through which the Indian Brahmin caste in the postcolonial period has appropriated the European ideology of Aryan superiority in order to subjugate the lower castes and women.

206. Loomba, Ania. "Shakespeare and Cultural Difference." In *Alternative Shakespeares*, vol. 2, ed. Terence Hawkes, 164–191. London: Routledge, 1996.

Loomba discusses diverse representations of otherness in Shakespeare and Renaissance culture. Drawing upon Haydn White's study of the difference between the "wild man" figure ("generally mute, outside civil society, and thus potentially a noble savage" [177]) and the "Barbarian" of the civilized East (excessive in language and dress, living "under an alien law, and ... therefore knowingly evil" [177]), she contrasts Caliban with Othello and Cleopatra. Loomba emphasizes the difficulty of theorizing a form of resistance for Caliban that is not merely a reflection of contradictions within European ideologies, and she suggests that Shakespeare's plays respond not only to European texts, "but also, implicitly, with what these outsiders were saying to Europeans" (188).

207. Mebane, John S. *Renaissance Magic and the Return of the Golden Age: The Occult Tradition and Marlowe, Jonson, and Shakespeare.* Lincoln: Univ. of Nebraska Press, 1989.

This book argues that occult philosophy carried to its logical extreme the Renaissance emphasis on the ability of human beings to reform their own personalities and the world around them. Mebane sees Renaissance magic as the culmination of the belief that the human artist emulates and assists God in seeking to restore to the fallen world its prelapsarian purity. Consequently, the chapter on *Tmp* (174–99) interprets Prospero's art as aligned with providence and seeking to promote the magical "sea-change" of individual self-purification and interpersonal harmony. Mebane believes that the artistic coherence of Shakespeare's play is founded upon the playwright's use of magic as a multi-leveled symbol: Prospero's art is, literally, Hermetic magic; it also symbolizes the civilizing power of humanist education and moral self-discipline; and it is, simultaneously, theatrical art. On each of these levels, Mebane concludes, Shakespeare qualifies his affirmation of the transformative power of art by acknowledging the limitations of fallen human nature.

208. Mowat, Barbara. "Prospero, Agrippa, and Hocus Pocus." *English Literary Renaissance* 11 (Autumn 1981): 281–303.

Mowat argues that considering Prospero as essentially a benevolent magus or an evil sorcerer unduly limits our response to this ambiguous figure. She points out that, although Prospero sometimes resembles an intellectual magus in the Hermetic/Neoplatonic tradition, he also resembles popular stage magicians and street-corner "jugglers," as well as the wizards of prose romances. Prospero's ambiguity, she maintains, intensifies our sense that *Tmp* is a combination of "seriousness and jest, of belief and skepticism" (283) and amplifies our sense of wonder concerning the ambiguities of human experience. See also Mowat (no. 76).

209. Orgel, Stephen. *The Illusion of Power: Political Theater in the English Renaissance.* Berkeley and Los Angeles: Univ. of California Press, 1975.

Orgel argues that in the 17th century the court masque increasingly constructed idealized images of the monarch's power to purify the realm through intellect, virtue, and heroism. He emphasizes that the ruler's power is portrayed as godlike, his will attaining the force of natural law. The section on *Tmp* (especially 44–49) discusses the play's conflation of ruler and artist and interprets the work as a meditation on the power of the mind to order reality. Orgel concludes that eventually the court masque contributed to the insulation of the Stuart monarchy from realistic perceptions of the attitudes of the governed. See also nos. 184 and 238 by Orgel.

210. Schmidgall, Gary. *Shakespeare and the Courtly Aesthetic.* Berkeley and

Los Angeles: Univ. of California Press, 1981.

This book is an interdisciplinary study of the political, social, and artistic milieu of *Tmp*. In chap. 1 (1–26), Schmidgall embraces Rabkin's conception of "complementarity" (see Rabkin [no. 82]) and suggests that *Tmp*'s engagement with the ideals and realities of the royal court was ambivalent. In chap. 2 (27–68) he argues that Shakespeare's renewed political optimism and his use of materials from romance, pastoral, tragicomedy, and court masque correlate with the intensification of royal patronage in 1604. Chap. 3 discusses *Tmp* as "civilizing art" (69–98) whose vision of social virtues is won through confrontation with those forces that threaten civilization. Schmidgall compares *Tmp* with *The Aeneid* in its emphasis on deliverance and reconciliation through the virtues of the ruler. Chap. 4 (99–153) discusses the elitist interest in allegorical spectacle; Prospero as virtuoso artist; the relation between perspective, illusion, and magic; and comic structure. In chap. 5 (154–85) Schmidgall argues that *Tmp* is "eminently political," treating such themes as "the nature of the ideal courtier, of the good (Ariel) and the bad (Caliban) apprentice or servant, and of the many-headed monster" (155). He emphasizes the play's political iconography, viewing the storm and the restoration of calm, for example, as political disorder and harmony. Chap. 6 (186–214) argues that *Tmp*'s characterization of Caliban is influenced by Renaissance discussion of monstrous vices: disobedience; sensual indulgence; ignorance; and violent, unrestrained emotion. Chap. 7 (215–62) surveys a range of literary and iconographic influences on Prospero and argues that he is an enlightened theatrical magician; authorial persona; and (by act 5) royal paragon of virtue who embodies Wisdom, Temperance, and Enlightened Rule. Schmidgall also suggests, however, that the interruption of the wedding masque introduces questions, expanded in the revels speech (4.1.146–63), concerning the relation between idealized courtly art and political realities. The conclusion (263–71) compares *Tmp* to Velázquez's painting *Las Meninas* in its self-reflexive analysis of the creative process.

211. Schneider, Ben Ross, Jr. " 'Are We Being Historical Yet?': Colonialist Interpretations of Shakespeare's *Tempest*." *Shakespeare Studies* 23 (1995): 120–45.

This essay argues that many interpretations of *Tmp* have focused upon colonialist discourse to the exclusion of other historical contexts. Attention to the discourses of ethics and government influential in the Renaissance, especially the works of Cicero and Seneca, Schneider believes, leads us to appreciate the climactic importance of Prospero's rational "renunciation of vengeance and his abjuration of magic" (124), acts that suggest a critique of Prospero's earlier withdrawal from responsibility and his subsequent efforts to maximize his power (including his conquest of the island). Embracing his dukedom as a responsible and benevolent ruler and seeking to practice the clemency invoked in the epilogue, the essay concludes, enable Prospero to enjoy spiritual freedom.

212. Smith, James. *"The Tempest."* In *Shakespearian and Other Essays*, ed. Edward M. Wilson, 159–261. Cambridge: Cambridge Univ. Press, 1974. Excerpt repr. in Bloom (no. 270).

Smith argues that Prospero's "revels" speech (4.1.146–63) epitomizes the essential dreamlike qualities of *Tmp* as a whole. He discusses the play's perplexing, contradictory versions of events, concluding that *Tmp* suggests that mortal experience is influenced by a supernatural order that will ultimately protect goodness and correct or destroy evil. He compares *Tmp* and its sources, including Antonio de Eslava's *Noches de Invierno* and several pamphlets on the colonization of Virginia, concluding that the play is distinguished by "elements of nature or reality" (227) that establish its beauty and its profundity. Smith also analyzes the complexities of Caliban's character, arguing that he is human, rather than demonic; he sees Prospero as a compound of virtues and mortal shortcomings. *Tmp* affirms, in Smith's view, that even humans with Caliban's monstrous vices possess rights, and *Tmp* criticizes Prospero's participation in the self-deceptive rationalizations of colonialist pamphlets such as Strachey's *True Reportory of the Wrack and Redemption of Sir Thomas Gates*. Despite his emphasis on the self-serving nature of the colonialist pamphlets, Smith hesitates to affirm that "colonialism is wholly or necessarily an evil" (25).

212a. Strier, Richard. "'I Am Power': Normal and Magical Politics in *The Tempest*." In *Writing and Political Engagement in Seventeenth-Century England*, ed. Derek Hirst and Richard Strier, 9–30. Cambridge: Cambridge Univ. Press, 1999.

Arguing that "the Renaissance idea of magic and the idea of colonial administration have the same fantasy content: namely, the idea of omnipotence" (16), this essay focuses on master-servant relationships in *Tmp*, both in the "normal," or courtly, realm and in the "magical" realm of the colonized island. Strier concludes that the play affirms the difficulties of exerting control over colonized populations and thus discourages imperialism. He acknowledges that the play can evoke a range of political responses, and he suggests that some readers may see *Tmp* as a critique of "normal" authoritarian politics.

213. Tudeau-Clayton, Margaret. *Jonson, Shakespeare, and Early Modern Virgil*. Cambridge: Cambridge Univ. Press, 1998.

This book's introduction (1–17) discusses cultural constructions of Virgil and of Shakespeare as "absolute, ideal and transcendent figure[s] of authority serving to underwrite the political structure in place" (14). Jonson, Tudeau-Clayton argues, affirms Virgil's authoritative status, whereas Shakespeare (ironically, for those who have constructed his work as "transcendent") undermines it. Chap. 6 (194–244) argues that *Tmp*'s disruption of authority is more radical than the affirmation of constitutional monarchy proposed by Hamilton (no. 198). Relying in part on the methods of deconstruction, Tudeau-Clayton analyzes the play's use of " 'noise' from 'below' " (198), especially in 1.1. and 4.1, as disruptive of the orderliness of symbolic forms; she argues that the wedding masque in 4.1 is Virgilian in its affirmation of the power of art and learning to control nature, and that the disruption of the masque is one of many ways that *Tmp* subverts the cultural and political authority traditionally ascribed to Virgil and sought by Prospero.

213a. Wells, Robin Headlam. " 'Rarer Action': *The Tempest*." Chap. 6 of *Shakespeare on Masculinity*, 177–206. Cambridge: Cambridge Univ. Press, 2000.

This chapter argues that *Tmp* is more concerned with establishing peace through dynastic marriage and the arts of civilization than with colonialism. Though conceding that "Prospero has an unpleasantly autocratic side to him" (192), Wells emphasizes that Prospero's renunciation of revenge and his use of music to establish order and harmony relate him to Orpheus, the archetypal civilizer of humankind. For Wells, Prospero renounces "the 'rough magic' of destructive vengeance and employs a gentler art" (195), just as King James I opposed militant Protestantism and sought to promote peace in Europe. When Prospero proclaims that "The rarer action is / In virtue than in vengeance" (5.1.27–28), Wells concludes, he is rejecting a narrow vision of masculinity as martial prowess and "redefining masculine *virtus*" (195) as incorporating the power to promote love and harmony. See also no. 242.

214. Welsford, Enid. "The Masque Transmuted." In *The Court Masque*, 324–49. 1927. Repr. New York: Russell and Russell, 1962.

This chapter discusses Shakespeare's transmutation of elements from the court masque in *A Midsummer Night's Dream* and *Tmp*. Welsford emphasizes *Tmp*'s masque-like elements: its mysterious setting; Prospero's similarity to the "masque presenter" (339); the play's vision of society as a "harmony of unequal parts" (341); its evocation of the ephemeral quality of art and of life; and its relative lack of dramatic conflict. Welsford argues that, even though *Tmp* deals with moral and spiritual conflicts and includes a greater awareness of evil than was normally included in the court masque, "Shakespeare is now hymning the victory instead of describing the battle, the lyrical element has almost usurped the place of drama" (340). This chapter includes sensitive commentary on *Tmp*'s poetry and stagecraft.

215. West, Robert H. "Ceremonial Magic in *The Tempest*." In *Shakespeare and the Outer Mystery*, 80–95. Lexington: Univ. of Kentucky Press, 1968.

This chapter discusses *Tmp* in the context of Renaissance theories of magic and pneumatology. West emphasizes the play's uncertainties: Prospero often appears benign; however, Shakespeare does not stress the relationship between Prospero's art and providence, and the magician's command of spirits would have been judged by orthodox theologians as damnable. West concludes that the play does not strictly conform either to contemporary theories of benevolent magic or to orthodox condemnations of it, and that Prospero's mysterious art is therefore of ambiguous moral and spiritual status.

216. Wilson, Richard. "Voyage to Tunis: New History and the Old World of *The Tempest*." *ELH* 64 (1997): 333–57.

This article argues that British involvement in the Mediterranean, especially north Africa, is a more important context for *Tmp* than colonization of the New World. Wilson suggests parallels between Prospero and Robert Dudley, whose career included both acts of piracy and the redemption of Europeans who had been enslaved by rival powers in the Mediterranean; Dudley also claimed a private island and named it "Dudleana." Drawing upon Bernard-Henry Lévy's study of French Algeria (in *Adventures on the Freedom Road* [London: Harvill Press, 1995]), this essay concludes that, given the complexities of international relations in this area, "someone could be implicated in colonialism 'without being a monster'" (252).

See also nos. 106a, 181, 182, 183, 184, 185, 185a, 222a, 222b, 223, 224, 229, 230, 234, 235, 239, 240, 241, 242, 243, 245, 255, 267, 270, 272, 273, 274, 276, 271a, 271b, 277.

D. Language and Linguistics.

217. McDonald, Russ. "Reading *The Tempest*." *Shakespeare Survey* 43 (for 1990): 15–28.

This essay analyzes *Tmp*'s versification, with emphasis on its recapitulation, its "acoustic and lexical echoes" (24) and its ellipses. McDonald argues that the effect of the verse is to tantalize us with hints of significance, yet deny us unambiguous meaning. Focusing on the text, he concludes, leads us to see that *Tmp* eludes the univocal ideological position sometimes attributed to it by new historicists and cultural materialists who focus upon the play's contexts rather than its aesthetic form.

See also nos. 196, 214, 221, 235, 237, 238a, 243, 270, 272.

E. Criticism.

218. Arthos, John. *Shakespeare's Use of Dream and Vision.* Totowa, N.J.: Rowman and Littlefield, 1977.

Arthos argues that dreams, ghosts, and visions in Shakespeare continually evoke awe and wonder and hint at the existence of a realm of transcendence. His chapter on *Tmp* (173–202) explores the ways in which the play intimates the existence of a power that Prospero serves and that controls events but which cannot ultimately be named or defined. Love, Arthos concludes, enables the characters to participate in this ineffable power.

219. Berger, Harry, Jr. "Miraculous Harp: A Reading of Shakespeare's *Tempest*." *Shakespeare Studies* 5 (1969): 253–83. Repr. in Berger, *Second World and Green World: Studies in Renaissance Fiction Making*, 147–85. Berkeley and Los Angeles: Univ. of California Press, 1988. Repr. in Bloom (no. 271).

This article criticizes traditional readings of *Tmp* (e.g., no. 237) that emphasize Prospero's altruism and his partial success in seeking to promote forgiveness, reconciliation, and spiritual renewal. Prospero's island, Berger argues, provides the magician an escape from harsh realities and enables his self-indulgent utopian fantasy of absolute, benevolent control over evil. Berger sees Ariel as a personification of Prospero's escapist aestheticism and Caliban as an embodiment of primitive human potential, including a longing for beauty that Prospero, who uses Caliban as a scapegoat for his own guilt, cannot acknowledge.

220. Bradshaw, Graham. *Misrepresentations: Shakespeare and the Materialists.* Ithaca: Cornell Univ. Press, 1993.

This book argues that Shakespeare offers complex analyses of unresolved ethical or political problems, not the unified ideological stance that Bradshaw believes some critics emphasize. (Cf. nos. 39, 191, 204.) He stresses, for example, that complexities of characterization and suggestive analogies (or "dramatic rhymes") such as those between Ferdinand and Caliban serve to raise and complicate questions rather than answer them. Prospero, Bradshaw insists, is more than an evil colonialist; Caliban transcends the category of natural slave. Commentary on *Tmp* appears in 64–70, 144–45, et passim.

221. Brower, Reuben A. "The Mirror of Analogy: *The Tempest.*" In *The Fields of Light: An Experiment in Critical Reading*, 95–122. New York: Oxford Univ. Press, 1951. Repr. Westport, Conn.: Greenwood Press, 1981. Repr. in Bloom (no. 100) and Graff and Phelan (no. 271a).

This essay argues that *Tmp* is unified by recurrent motifs—"strange-wondrous," "sleep-and-dream," "sea-tempest," "music-and-noise," "earth-air," "slavery-freedom," "and "sovereignty-conspiracy" (97)—that establish a system of analogies among dramatic experiences. Through close readings of passages such as Ariel's song "Full Fathom Five" (1.2.397–405), Alonzo's repentance scene (3.3), and Prospero's revels speech (4.1.146–63), Brower demonstrates that these motifs are unified by the central metaphor of "sea change," or magical transformation, and he relates them to plot structure and to psychological and moral metamorphoses of characters. Brower's essay is among the most helpful and influential formalist analyses of this play.

222. Coletti, Theresa. "Music and *The Tempest.*" In Tobias and Zolbrod (no. 109), 185–99.

This essay discusses the thematic and structural functions of music in *Tmp*. Coletti interprets Prospero's music not simply as a reflection of cosmic harmony, but also as a means of bringing characters toward recognition of their disorders and thus providing an opportunity for regeneration that each person must accept or reject. Ariel's song "Full Fathom Five" (1.2.397–405), for example, both suggests the possibility of reforming mortal imperfections and invites Ferdinand to contribute to the regenerative process. Coletti contrasts orderly and disorderly music in *Tmp* and emphasizes the tenuousness of the order that Prospero strives, with considerable difficulty, to effect. For a comprehensive catalogue of music related to *Tmp*, see vol. 3 of *A Shakespeare Music Catalogue*, ed. Bryan N. S. Gooch and David Thatcher (Oxford: Clarendon Press, 1991); vol. 5 is a selected bibliography on Shakespeare and music.

222a. Coursen, H. R. *The Tempest: A Guide to the Play.* Greenwood Guides to Shakespeare. Westport, Conn.: Greenwood Press, 2000.

This book provides students with a survey and evaluation of scholarship and criticism on *Tmp*, as well as Coursen's critical commentary. Coursen begins with chapters on "Textual History" (1–6) and "Contexts and Sources" (7–43), including discussion of the romance tradition, court masques, magic, and science. The chapter on "Dramatic Structure" (45–62) provides scene-by-scene commentary. In "Themes" (63–78) Coursen defends formalist criticism; discusses such themes as power, the sea, and the clash of religious and ratio-nalalist world views; and argues that *Tmp* is "more capable of supporting radically opposed points of view than Macbeth" (66). Coursen's survey of "Critical Approaches" (79–140) begins with Ben Jonson and proceeds through postmodernism, including sections on new criticism, feminism, generic criti-cism, linguistic approaches, psychological criticism and character analyses, varieties of historicism, colonialist criticism, and theological approaches. "The Play in Performance" (141–95) analyzes numerous stage performan-ces, films, and video productions of *Tmp* and its offshoots; Coursen ar-gues that there can be no definitive interpretation or performance. In the "Bibliographical Essay" (197–99) Coursen comments upon the scholarship and criticism that he finds most useful. The chapter on performance, with its sensitive appreciation of the play's theatrical values and its assessments of directors' and actors' visions of *Tmp*, is a major strength of this volume.

222b. Cox, John D. "Recovering Something Christian about *The Tem-pest.*" *Christianity and Literature* 50 (2000): 31–51.

This article argues that both Prospero and Caliban are complex human characters whose "ability to improve in goodness, a grace-be-stowed human characteristic" (44) is best understood through the ethical system of Christianity. Cox emphasizes that, despite the faults of Pros-pero, his forgiveness of his enemies cannot be dismissed as motivated by self-interest, since he could easily have achieved his political objectives by destroying them; Cox also stresses Caliban's decision to "seek for grace" (5.1.296) and Prospero's leaving the island in Caliban's possession. Cox distinguishes this interpretation from new historicist and cultural material-ist readings that stereotype Prospero as evil colonialist and from idealist readings that allegorize Caliban as the embodiment of evil. The essay provides an assessment of the presuppositions, insights, and shortcomings of previous criticism (including Kermode [no. 182], Orgel [no. 184], and Barker and Hulme [no. 187]), and it offers incisive commentary on Prospero, Caliban, and other characters.

223. Felperin, Howard. "Early Utopian Discourse." In Felperin (no. 101), 122–41.

Drawing upon Paul de Man's theory of deconstruction, Felperin criti-cizes the effort of Barker and Hulme (no. 187) to evade historical relativ-ism and assert that colonialist discourse is dominant in *Tmp*. Felperin then argues that the formal structure of *Tmp*, like that of More's Utopia and Montaigne's "Of the Cannibals," is founded upon a dialectic between an imperialist discourse that affirms the dominant political authority and a utopian discourse that subverts it. He cites as examples Gonzalo's interrupted utopian speech (4.1), Prospero's abortive masque (4.1), and "Miranda's fleeting impression of a brave new world" in 5.1.180–84 (141). See also no. 224.

224. Felperin, Howard. "Political Criticism at the Crossroads: The Utopian Historicism of *The Tempest*." In Wood (no. 278), 29–66.

This essay initially discusses the opposition between formalist criticism and materialist/new historicist approaches; the former typically affirms a vision of "essential human nature" (34) and transcendent value, while the latter seek to demystify a text by revealing its ideological function within a specific culture. Felperin proposes to reconcile the two approaches in a "larger view" (33) based on Fredric Jameson's belief that criticism may reveal not only oppressive ideological elements but also liberating utopian ones. Assessing critiques of *Tmp*'s colonialist ideology as partial, Felperin argues that Prospero's "revels" speech (4.1.146–63) envisions a future in which all systems of political domination and material possessiveness will disappear. Although Felperin says that we cannot specify whether this future event is "the Christian apocalypse, ... a revolutionary utopia" or "something else," he affirms the value of this prophecy of "a collective destiny ... that throws into relief and into insignificance the clash of factional agendas that have held the stage up to now" (58).

225. Felperin, Howard. "Romance and Romanticism: Some Reflections on *The Tempest* and *Heart of Darkness*, or When Is Romance No Longer Romance?" In Kay and Jacobs (no. 102), 60–76. Repr. in *Critical Inquiry* 6 (1980): 691–706, and, with revisions, in no. 101.

Felperin interprets *Tmp* and Conrad's *Heart of Darkness* as dramatizing an unresolved "dialectic between the demystification and remystification of their own romance mode" (76). He criticizes interpretations of *Tmp* as univocally affirming redemption (e.g., nos. 61, 71, 72, 84, 85). Drawing on Berger (no. 219), Felperin emphasizes Prospero's faults and the self-interestedness of his art, yet he also suggests that Prospero's renunciation of magic is "a self-humiliation into humanity that redresses his earlier self-exaltation in art" (67). Thus, Felperin concludes, the play's demystification of romance and magic results paradoxically in the affirmation of the power of another form of art.

226. Fox-Good, Jacquelyn. "Other Voices: The Sweet, Dangerous Air(s) of Shakespeare's *Tempest.*" *Shakespeare Studies* 24 (1996): 241–74.

This article criticizes the traditional tendency to associate music exclusively with transcendent harmony and order, arguing instead that music in *Tmp* often evokes "the body in its most threatening forms, as sexual, as female, as beastly, or deformed" (263). Fox-Good defends this interpretation through analysis of scores for "Full Fathom Five" (1.2.397–405) and "Where the Bee Sucks" (5.1.87–94) written by Robert Johnson for Shakespeare's company. She also argues that *Tmp* describes music as "dispersed, fluid, marginal" (254) and thus as a feminine subtext that disrupts Prospero's efforts to maintain a patriarchal order. Fox-Good criticizes assumptions about music in idealist readings of *Tmp* such as that of Knight (no. 72) and in new historicist criticism, including work by Brown (no. 190).

227. Holland, Peter. "The Shapeliness of *The Tempest.*" *Essays in Criticism* 45 (1995): 208–29.

Drawing on Mark Rose's *Shakespearean Design* (Cambridge: Harvard Univ. Press, 1972), this article analyzes parallels among scenes in *Tmp*'s nine-scene structure. Holland emphasizes that scene five (3.1), the log-bearing scene in which Ferdinand and Miranda display genuine love for each other, is, despite the imperfect character of *Tmp*'s final resolution, the play's "triumphant centre" (226).

228. Hunt, John S. "Prospero's Empty Grasp." *Shakespeare Studies* 22 (1994): 277–313.

Hunt discusses *Tmp*'s response to Renaissance dreams of intellectual mastery of experience and physical conquest of the earth. He argues that Shakespeare's characters are presented with opportunities to acknowledge the limitations of their powers and to find a more fulfilling selfhood in human community. Although Prospero strives to frustrate his enemies' grasping for power, Hunt maintains, the major thrust of *Tmp* is to humble Prospero, who learns (especially through the intrusion of reality into the masque in 4.1) that he is isolated from human realities as he attempts in vain to escape mortality through magic. The essay concludes that Prospero's renunciation of his art leads him toward a community made possible by the mutual dependency and forgiveness that he humbly requests in the epilogue.

229. James, D[avid] G[wilym]. *The Dream of Prospero.* Oxford: Clarendon Press, 1967.

James begins (chap. 1, 1–26) by suggesting that *Tmp* goes beyond the vision of ineradicable evil we find in *Hamlet* and *King Lear*. He then emphasizes (chap. 2, 27–44) that the storm exists on two levels, a level of illusion experienced by Miranda and of greater understanding possessed by Prospero. Chap. 3 (45–71) argues that *Tmp* consigns magic to the realm of the fanciful, so that Prospero's farewell to his art is the farewell of the European mind to the magical tradition founded upon Hermetic and Neoplatonic sources. After extensive discussion relating *Tmp* to Renaissance literature of exploration, chap. 4 (72–123) argues that, while Prospero sees only the brute in Caliban, Shakespeare reveals that this primitive character possesses a "sense of dependence on a transcendent world" (114) that can be attenuated by civilization. Chap. 5 (124–53) stresses that Prospero has embarked on a journey toward spiritual perfection, and that his return to Milan dramatizes the necessity of founding civilization upon a quest for spiritual awareness. James describes *Tmp* as a dream of human existence that reveals the relation between worldly affairs and religious and moral ideals. In chap. 6 (154–74), James discusses the influence of the court masque on *Tmp*, and he suggests that the play contains mysterious intimations of spiritual realities, including the suggestion that Prospero is both a human character and an embodiment of providence.

230. Kernan, Alvin. *The Playwright as Magician: Shakespeare's Image of the Poet in the English Public Theater.* New Haven: Yale Univ. Press, 1979.

This book studies the evolution of Shakespeare's conception of dramatic art in relation to Renaissance concepts of the poet as moral and spiritual teacher and in response to the constraints of the Elizabethan public theater. Chaps. 6 and 7 (129–59) discuss Prospero's island as an imaginary, almost idealized theater, free of the limits of the public playhouse, in which the playwright/magician enacts fictions that have the power to reform their audiences. Yet *Tmp* is ambivalent, Kernan argues, about the power of art: Shakespeare suggests that plays can bring their viewers toward knowledge of the world, of themselves, and of moral ideals, yet Prospero is also aware of the contingency of his artistic vision and of the shortcomings of the audience, some of whom lack sufficient imagination to participate in the artist's vision.

231. Knights, L. C. "*The Tempest.*" In Tobias and Zolbrod (no. 109), 15–31.

Knights discusses Prospero's renunciation of his art as part of his quest for renewal of self. He argues that *Tmp* uses masque and music, as well as Gonzalo's utopianism in 2.1, to hint at an ideal realm that eludes us as we confront the difficulties and contradictions of our mortal lives.

232. Kott, Jan. "Prospero's Staff." In *Shakespeare Our Contemporary,* trans. Boleslaw Taborski, 293–341. London: Methuen, 1964. Repr. New York: Norton, 1974. Repr. in no. 274.

Kott argues that the structure of *Tmp* is based on multiple plots that dramatize variations on a unifying theme that is an epitome of world history: the struggle for power that manifests itself in violent usurpation. In order to dramatize actions that mirror an essential aspect of the real world, Kott believes, Shakespeare created a symbolic island that cannot be identified simply with the New World. The play as a whole, he concludes, bitterly refutes Gonzalo's utopianism (2.1), as well as the views of critics who view the island as an Arcadia.

233. Lindenbaum, Peter. "Prospero's Anger." *The Massachusetts Review* 75 (Spring 1984): 161–71.

This article argues that Prospero's habitual anger is an expression of his frustration at having to live in a fallen world characterized by those human failings that the magician finally confesses he shares with Caliban. Lindenbaum sees Prospero's successful struggle to accept his own limitations as a corollary of *Tmp*'s advocacy of meaningful action in the fallen world, as opposed to withdrawal into contemplation.

234. Marx, Leo. "Shakespeare's American Fable." In *The Machine in the Garden: Technology and the Pastoral Ideal in America*, 34–72. New York: Oxford Univ. Press, 1964.

This chapter argues that *Tmp* "prefigures the design of the classic American fables, and especially the idea of a redemptive journey away from society in the direction of nature" (69). Comparing the play to its sources in Montaigne's "Of the Cannibals" and in Renaissance travel literature, Marx analyzes the oscillation in *Tmp* between two different visions of the New World, and consequently nature itself. The first of these is a vision of nature as an unspoiled garden or golden world (as in Gonzalo's utopian speeches of 2.1); the second, more frightening, vision is the image of nature as savage wilderness (as suggested by the storm that opens the play and by the negative aspects of Caliban). Marx concludes that *Tmp* expresses the hope that human art can ameliorate society by controlling destructive tendencies in nature and reforming the corruptions of civilization; Prospero's island is thus a pastoral retreat in which "the superfluities and defenses of everyday life are stripped away, and men regain contact with essentials" (69). This study provides balanced and sensitive commentary on *Tmp*'s structure, characterization, and poetry, as well as its place in cultural history.

235. Norbrook, David. "'What Cares These Roarers for the Name of

King?': Language and Utopia in *The Tempest.*" In *The Politics of Tragicomedy: Shakespeare and After*, ed. Gordon McMullan and Jonathan Hope, 21–54. London: Routledge, 1992. Repr. in Ryan (no. 106b) and White (no. 277a).

This essay argues that "the writer as agent" can "achieve a degree of independence from the prevailing structures of power and discourse" (25). Norbrook argues that *Tmp* provides a critical analysis of utopian discourse and a skeptical (though not cynical) response to Prospero's hope for restoration of a stable dynasty. He also maintains that Shakespeare builds upon Montaigne's critique of the idea that hierarchy is inherent in nature. Responding to Greenblatt (no. 196), Norbrook stresses the conflicts within and among discourses of colonialism, and he affirms that Caliban's subjectivity is not fully confined by his master's language.

236. Nuttall, A[nthony] D[avid]. *Two Concepts of Allegory: A Study of Shakespeare's "The Tempest" and the Logic of Allegorical Expression.* London: Routledge; New York: Barnes and Noble, 1967.

Following a survey (1–14) of allegorical readings of *Tmp*, Nuttall devotes two chapters (15–72) to the metaphysical and psychological tendencies that underlie different types of allegory. He then argues (chap. 4, 73–107) that in the Renaissance artists and poets saw "the ideal not as separated from the here-and-now but as interpenetrating it" (81). This leads (chap. 5, 108–35) to discussion of the spiritual dimensions of love as "the experience of supreme value" (134) in Shakespeare, especially in the sonnets. Chap. 6 (136–58) argues that *Tmp* is not an allegory in which characters and events are clearly assigned a spiritual or psychological meaning, yet the play nonetheless hints at metaphysical levels of significance, such as the suggestion that "Love is ... a supernatural force" (160). We are tempted to lend these hints credence, Nuttall believes, because of the play's combination of realism and transcendentalism, yet the play's "regress of fictions" (146), its dissolving of the distinction between dreams and reality, also suggests the possible validity of different perspectives upon human experience.

237. Orgel, Stephen. "New Uses of Adversity: Tragic Experience in *The Tempest.*" In *In Defense of Reading: A Reader's Approach to Literary Criticism*, ed. Reuben Brower and Richard Poirier, 110–32. New York: Dutton, 1962.

This article argues that Prospero "leads the play ... through suffering to reconciliation and a new life" (125). For Orgel, the artistic vision of *Tmp* does not exclude the tragic elements of experience, but it brings them into relation with the vision of natural order that is adumbrated in Prospero's masque (4.1). This vision of order, Orgel suggests, is juxtaposed to a sense of life's dangers and misfortunes. Orgel comments frequently on styles of poetry in *Tmp* in relation to structure and theme. For Orgel's revision of this interpretation, see nos. 184, 209, and 238. For further commentary, see no. 219.

238. Orgel, Stephen. "Prospero's Wife." *Representations* 8 (1984): 1–13. Repr. in *Rewriting the Renaissance: The Discourse of Sexual Difference in Early Modern Europe*, ed. Margaret Ferguson, Maureen Quilligan, and Nancy J. Vickers, 50–64. Chicago: Univ. of Chicago Press, 1986. Repr. in Bloom (no. 271).

Orgel uses a psychoanalytical approach to explore patriarchal assumptions in the text and its reception history. Denying the stability of the text, he argues that plays are "collaborative fantasies" created by authors, theater ensembles, and audiences. The almost complete absence of Prospero's wife creates a space, Orgel suggests, that not only Prospero but commentators and editors have filled with imaginary corrupt wives and mothers and powerful fathers. The essay emphasizes Prospero's need to maintain power over a usurping younger brother, rather than his commitment to forgiveness and reconciliation. See also nos. 184 and 209 by Orgel. For commentary, see no. 238a.

238a. Pierce, Robert B. "Understanding *The Tempest*." *New Literary History* 30 (1999): 373–88.

Drawing upon Ludwig Wittgenstein's philosophy of language, Pierce argues that there is no "series of true statements" (377) that constitutes the meaning of a play, nor is there a single goal in the process of interpretation. For Pierce, understanding a play entails a range of skills: seeing "connections among different parts of the play" (379), appreciating complexities of character, and acquiring the ability to read lines meaningfully, among others. Evaluating a range of different perspectives on *Tmp*—notably the formalist, the new historical/colonialist, and the feminist—Pierce finds many of them illuminating, yet he criticizes some as failing to illuminate his own experience. He thus concludes that meaning "is not independent of the reader or viewer" (379). This article comments judiciously on the interpretations of Tillyard (no. 84), Orgel (nos. 184 and 238), Barker and Hulme (no. 187), Greenblatt (no. 196), Leininger (no. 204), Driscoll (in no. 271), and others.

239. Skura, Meredith Anne. "Discourse and the Individual: The Case of Colonialism in *The Tempest*." *SQ* 40 (1989): 42–69. Repr. in nos. 270, 271a, and 276.

While acknowledging the influence of the discourse of colonialism on

Tmp, Skura emphasizes the dangers of interpreting the play exclusively in relation to the collective political unconscious and ignoring the unique voice of an artist who shapes culture as well as being shaped by it. As an alternative to the political analyses of new historicists and cultural materialists (e.g., nos. 187, 190, 196), she develops a psychoanalytical reading of the play: Prospero's wrathful condemnation of Caliban is the product of the magician's projection of his own imperfectly repressed vengefulness, will to power, and sensuality onto a subordinate character. Skura suggests that *Tmp* provides a critical analysis of Prospero's will to power rather than simply affirming his complicity with colonial ideology.

240. Traister, Barbara Howard. *Heavenly Necromancers: The Magician in English Renaissance Drama.* Columbia: Univ. of Missouri Press, 1984. Excerpt on *Tmp* repr. in Bloom (no. 271).

Traister discusses the influences of Neoplatonic magic, medieval romance, Renaissance epic, and popular belief on Renaissance plays about magic. Her chapter on *Tmp* (125–49) stresses Prospero's similarity to the playwright as he presents a series of magical/theatrical illusions designed to teach self-knowledge, foster Ferdinand and Miranda's love, and restore social harmony. Traister argues that Prospero is predominantly benevolent; his renunciation of his art expresses his commitment to retaining his humanity, rather than striving to be godlike. For Traister, Prospero's power as a magician and (paradoxically) his awareness of his limitations make him a "master of self-knowledge" who strives—with mixed success—to stimulate similar self-awareness in other characters.

241. Turner, John. "Reading by Contraries: *The Tempest* as Romance." In Wood (no. 278), 97–126.

Drawing upon Bruno Bettelheim's theory of the psychoanalytical function of fairy tales and Bronislaw Malinowski's analysis of the social functions of myth, this essay explores the tensions in *Tmp* between (1) elements of romance and of folklore, both of which have roots "in general existential predicaments," and (2) "historically specific" problems of political hierarchy and control (107). Turner argues that *Tmp* provides a dream of psychic and social integration and simultaneously acknowledges the intractable nature of the conflicts that the dream/romance would resolve. He concludes that this conflict between an awareness of discordant reality and a fantasy of peace and virtue give *Tmp* its "peculiar poignancy" (123).

242. Wells, Robin Headlam. "Prospero, King James and the Myth of the

Musician-King." In *Elizabethan Mythologies: Studies in Poetry, Drama, and Music*, 63–80. Cambridge: Cambridge Univ. Press, 1994.

This chapter argues that *Tmp* "demands that we consider the contingent nature of the myths that form the basis of our sense of political reality" (64). *Tmp*'s portrait of Prospero, Wells believes, simultaneously dramatizes the myth of the musician-king as creator of social harmony and warns the monarch against neglect of his responsibilities. Wells then analyzes the ways that the play calls attention to its own fictive status, concluding that it does not affirm a rational order so much as suggest that human faith and action may make order possible. Wells responds judiciously to new historicist and poststructuralist criticism, maintaining that *Tmp* participates in multiple discourses and that no single critical approach is exhaustive. See also no. 231a.

243. Young, David. " 'Where the Bee Sucks': A Triangular Study of *Doctor Faustus, The Alchemist*, and *The Tempest*." In Kay and Jacobs (no. 102), 149–66.

Young contrasts the treatments of language, decorum, dramatic illusion, and stagecraft in *Doctor Faustus, The Alchemist*, and *Tmp*. He sees *Tmp* as an effort to retain some of the exuberance of Marlowe's style and dramatic method while acknowledging Jonson's "healthy skepticism about linguistic potency" (152) and his insistence on decorum (as reflected in *Tmp*'s observation of the classical unities of time and place).

F. Stage History; Performance Criticism; Film and Television Versions.

244. Brook, Peter, director. Ian Wilson, producer. *Peter Brook: The Tempest.* Saga Films (Paris), 1968.

Aimed at college and university theater students, this film discusses and illustrates methods for directing *Tmp*. For additional information see no. 23, item 615.

245. Demaray, John G. *Shakespeare and the Spectacles of Strangeness: "The Tempest" and the Transformation of Renaissance Theatrical Forms.* Pittsburgh: Duquesne Univ. Press, 1998.

This study analyzes *Tmp*'s genre, structure, and symbolism in the context of the theatrical conditions at Whitehall in 1611–13. The introduction (1–16) suggests that these conditions encouraged Shakespeare to construct a "masque-like iconographic cosmos" (13) as the play's setting. Chap. 1 (17–43) argues that the play is a unique compound of elements from the court masque; narrative and dramatic romance, pastoral, and tragicomedy; and vestiges of four-part Latin drama. In chap. 2 (44–65) Demaray argues that *Tmp* balances "episodes of antic disorder against final Triumphs of social integration" (60); the visionary betrothal masque, for example, moves toward a final resolution that, though postponed by Caliban's conspiracy, is consummated in Prospero's magical unmasking and reconciliation of the principal characters. Shakespeare qualifies the play's idealization of the social order, Demaray adds, through an epilogue that reveals the ruler's mortal limitations. Chap. 3 (73–93) discusses such scenes as the descent of Juno and the dissolution of the masque in 4.1 in relation to the theatrical machinery and conventions of court performances. Chaps. 4 and 5 (101–34) argue that *Tmp*'s symbolism expresses the conflict between utopian fantasies and mortal imperfections. Demaray contrasts Gonzalo's egalitarian fantasy and Caliban's longing for a material paradise with Prospero's betrothal masque, with its emphasis on "cool, restrained, chaste love" (122). He argues that *Tmp*'s conclusion juxtaposes "ideals of innocence" (134) and the invocation of divine providence with an awareness of mortals' capacity for violence and treachery. The epilogue (135–38) argues that *Tmp* is a "pivotal" work in theater history, anticipating the Restoration emphasis upon music, dance, and exotic spectacles. Throughout this book Demaray is critical of ideological readings (e.g., nos. 187, 190) that he believes take insufficient account of the play's aesthetic structure. The volume includes seventeen illustrations (66–72, 94–100).

246. Gorrie, John, director. Cedric Messina, producer. *The Tempest.* The BBC "Shakespeare Plays" Series, 1979.

This production often develops masque-like qualities against a simple, stylized background setting. Most of the text of *Tmp* is preserved, but there are some cuts and rearrangements. The cast includes Michael Hordern (Prospero), Warren Clarke (Caliban), David Dixon (Ariel), and Pippa Guard (Miranda). Reviewers have typically found this television version competent but not distinguished. Available from The Writing Company and elsewhere. For further information and commentary, see no. 24, item 620.

247. Hirst, David L. *The Tempest.* Text and Performance. General ed. Michael Scott. London: Macmillan, 1984.

This book provides an introduction to *Tmp* through literary and performance criticism. Part 1 (9–40) argues that the play is ambiguous in its treatment of art and nature and emphasizes that Prospero fails to achieve fully his project—to establish a harmony on earth that mirrors that of the heavens. Part 2 (41–68) discusses *Tmp*'s performance history, with emphasis on productions directed by Jonathan Miller (Mermaid Theatre, 1970);

Peter Hall (National Theatre, 1974); Giorgio Strehler (Piccolo Teatro, Milan, Italy, 1978); and the film version by Derek Jarman (1980, no. 249). Hirst contrasts John Gielgud's performance of the speech in which Prospero renounces his art (5.1.33–57, recorded on his album *Ages of Man*) and that of Heathcote Williams in Jarman's film; he then surveys contrasting treatments of the issue of colonialism, conceptions of magic, and theatrical spectacle.

248. Jackson, Russell. "Shakespeare's Comedies on Film." In *Shakespeare and the Moving Image: The Plays on Film and Television,* ed. Anthony Davies and Stanley Wells, 99–120. Cambridge: Cambridge Univ. Press, 1994.

This essay includes a contrastive analysis (107–10) of Derek Jarman's *Tmp* (1980; no. 249) and Peter Greenaway's *Prospero's Books* (1991; no. 259). Jackson concludes that Jarman's film updates *Tmp*'s fantasy through "costume, lighting and set-dressing rather than filmic tricks" (109), whereas Greenaway provides an extravagantly illustrated commentary on the play rather than the story itself.

249. Jarman, Derek, director. Don Boyd, Sarah Radclyffe, Guy Ford, and Mordecai Schreiber, producers. *The Tempest, by William Shakespeare, as Seen through the Eyes of Derek Jarman.* World Northal Films, British Films Now series (New York), 1980.

This film uses somewhat more than half of Shakespeare's text, although there is much rearrangement. Jarman's rendition of *Tmp* creates an atmosphere of nightmare; reviewers have disagreed sharply, some finding Jarman's film repulsive, others praising its innovative vision. For further information and commentary, see no. 24, item 622; and nos. 247, 248, 272.

250. Schaefer, George, director and producer. *The Tempest.* Hallmark Hall of Fame, 1960.

This production features Richard Burton (Caliban), Maurice Evans (Prospero), Roddy McDowall (Ariel), and Lee Remick (Miranda). Although cut to 76 minutes and taped in black and white, this television version has been highly praised as faithful to the spirit of Shakespeare's play and appropriate for high school students as well as more mature audiences. Available from The Writing Company. For further information and commentary, see no. 24, item 613.

251. Woodman, William, director. Joseph Papp, producer. *The Tempest.* Bard Productions Shakespeare Series, 1985.

This 126–minute film features Efrem Zimbalist, Jr. (Prospero), William H. Bassett (Alonso), J. E. Taylor (Miranda), Duane Black (Ariel),

William Hootkins (Caliban), and Edward Edwards (Sebastian). The Bard series is designed to compete with the BBC Shakespeare Plays in its effort to appeal to broad audiences. Available from The Writing Company and elsewhere. For additional information, see no. 24, item 627.

See also nos. 183, 184, 185a, 189, 209, 214, 222a,
259, 261, 262, 267, 271b.

G. Reception History; Adaptations and Commentary on Adaptations; The Tempest as Source for and Influence on Later Writers and Works.

252. Auden, W. H. "The Sea and the Mirror: A Commentary on Shakespeare's *The Tempest.*" 1944. Repr. in *Collected Longer Poems*, 199–252. New York: Random House, 1969. Also in *Collected Poems*, ed. Edward Mendelson, 309–41. New York: Random House, 1976. Excerpt repr. in Palmer (no. 274).

Auden's poem takes the form of an imaginary dialogue among Shakespeare's characters after the conclusion of a performance of *Tmp*. The poem reflects upon the purposes of art, especially in relation to the natural world and the development of religious faith. For commentary, see nos. 93, 270, 272.

253. Bamber, Linda. "Claribel at Palace Dot Tunis." In Novy (no. 264), 237–57.

This epistolary short story takes the form of fictional letters and email messages from Miranda to Claribel. Through this fiction, Bamber provides speculation concerning the lives of *Tmp*'s characters after the play's conclusion (and after their transposition into a modern setting); reflections upon *Tmp*'s psychological, cultural, and political significance; and delightfully witty responses to the play's reception history, the state of modern Shakespearean criticism, and aspects of modern culture.

254. Browning, Robert. "Caliban upon Setebos." 1864. Repr. in *Complete Works of Robert Browning*, ed. John C. Berkey, Allan C. Dooley, and Susan E. Dooley, 6: 259–70. Waco, Tex.: Baylor Univ. Press; Athens, Ohio: Ohio Univ. Press, 1996.

In this dramatic monologue, Browning's Caliban reflects upon the nature of his God, Setebos; the poem thus suggests Browning's analysis of the history of religion and his critique of anthropomorphism. For commentary see nos. 93, 267, 270, 272.

255. Cartelli, Thomas. *Repositioning Shakespeare: National Formations, Postcolonial Appropriations.* London: Routledge, 1999.

This book's introduction (1–23) discusses the purposes and the political significance of appropriations of Shakespeare in postcolonial cultures. As part of Cartelli's analysis of Shakespeare's influence in the United States (27–83), chap. 3 (63–83) interprets Percy MacKaye's *Caliban by the Yellow Sands*, a masque performed in New York over a ten-day period in 1916. Cartelli emphasizes the contradiction between the "democratic claims advanced [by MacKaye and others] on behalf of the masque and the largely anti-democratic bias of its themes and organization" (74), especially its implication that immigrants from non Anglo-Saxon cultures (apparently symbolized by Caliban) must adopt the allegedly superior Anglo-American culture embodied in Prospero if the United States is to maintain its position of cultural and political leadership in the world. Chap. 4 (87–104) analyzes interpretations of *Tmp* by authors (e.g., the Kenyan Ngugi Wa Thiong'o and the West Indian George Lamming) in several former European colonies. Although Cartelli concedes that *Tmp* may possess considerable ideological complexity and self-contradiction, he nonetheless argues that the play's characterizations of Caliban and Prospero reveal an ethnocentric vision that defines human civilization as distinctively European and the colonized alien as an evil, intractable student, rather than seeing the possibility of forms of otherness that deserve respect. Shakespeare himself, Cartelli concludes, is thus complicit in the tradition of colonialist ideology in which the play participates. (Chap. 4 is a revised version of "Prospero in Africa: The Tempest as Colonialist Text and Pretext," in *Shakespeare Reproduced: The Text in History and Ideology*, ed. Jean E. Howard and Marion F. O'Connor [New York: Methuen, 1987], 99–115. For commentary, see no. 205.) Chap. 5 (105–19) argues that *No Telephone to Heaven* (1989), by Jamaican-American novelist Michelle Cliff, progresses beyond many postcolonial works in the extent to which it transforms Eurocentric premises concerning power and gender. Following a section on *Othello* (123–68), the conclusion (169–180) discusses Nadine Gordimer's *My Son's Story* (1990) and Robert Stone's *Children of Light* (1986), suggesting that Shakespeare's plays may be appropriated for purposes that are not "underwritten by any particular national or cultural agenda" (174).

256. Césaire, Aimé. *Une Tempête.* Paris: Seuil, 1969. Extract repr. in Hulme and Sherman (no. 271b).

Césaire's play, written for an all-black cast, portrays Caliban as a heroic, rebellious slave and Prospero as totalitarian European conqueror. Written by a native of Martinique, *Une Tempête* illustrates the appropriation of Shakespeare's play in anticolonialist literature. For commentary, see nos. 93, 255, 265, 267, 271b.

257. Coursen, H[erbert] R. " 'Tis Nudity': Peter Greenaway's *Prospero's Books.*" In *Watching Shakespeare on Television*, 163–76. Rutherford, N.J.: Fairleigh Dickinson Univ. Press; London: Associated Univ. Presses, 1993.

Coursen argues that *Prospero's Books* (no. 259) is incoherent: Greenaway's combination of allusions to the story of *Tmp*, speeches by a narrator, and digressions into books assumed to be the play's sources fails to illuminate Shakespeare's work or create a meaningful aesthetic experience. Coursen also criticizes such techniques as Greenaway's occasional imposition of a television screen onto the film.

258. Donaldson, Peter S. "Shakespeare in the Age of Post-Mechanical Reproduction: Sexual and Electronic Magic in *Prospero's Books.*" In *Shakespeare, the Movie: Popularizing the Plays on Film, TV, and Video*, ed. Lynda E. Boose and Richard Burt, 169–85. London: Routledge, 1997.

Drawing heavily upon Peter Greenaway's published script, this essay argues that *Prospero's Books* (no. 259) analyzes the creative power of modern technology as an extension of Renaissance magic. For Donaldson, this film extends the interpretations of Adelman (no. 50) and Kay Stockholder (unpublished paper, 1989) that see Prospero's magic as an effort to appropriate feminine reproductive capacities. Donaldson concludes that many aspects of Greenaway's interpretation of *Tmp* appear, ironically, "only in the book" (183).

259. Greenaway, Peter, director. Kees Kasander, producer. *Prospero's Books.* Miramax Films, 1991. Script by Greenaway published as *Prospero's Books: A Film of Shakespeare's "The Tempest."* New York: Four Walls Eight Windows, 1991.

Although Greenaway has described this film as an effort to turn Shakespeare's text into images, most commentators have regarded it either as a commentary on *Tmp* or as a new work inspired in part by Shakespeare's play. Fragments of the text of *Tmp* are spoken by John Gielgud while layers of imagery ostensibly explore the books Prospero has brought to his island. This work combines "postmodern" intellectual interests and sensational visual effects, including extensive nudity and an occasional vivisection. Some reviewers have recoiled from the sensationalism of this film, but others admire its avant-garde methods and its commentary on *Tmp*'s conscious and subconscious sources and effects. For commentary, see nos. 248, 257, 258, 261, 262, 272.

260. Guffey, George Robert, ed. *After "The Tempest."* Augustan Reprint Society. Special Series, no. 4. Los Angeles: William Andrews Clark Memorial Library, 1969.

This volume includes facsimile reprints of William Davenant and John Dryden's *The Tempest, or The Enchanted Island* (performed 1667; pub. 1670); the operatic version produced by Thomas Shadwell and others (1674); Thomas Duffett's *Mock Tempest, or the Enchanted Castle* (performed 1674; pub. 1675); and *The Tempest, An Opera* (1756), possibly by David Garrick. Guffey's introduction discusses the authorship of these works and relationships among them and Shakespeare's *Tmp*; notes that Furness (no. 181) reprints Shadwell's 1674 version and refers to it erroneously as the original Dryden-Davenant work; and assesses the influence of Shakespeare's *Tmp* on Fletcher's *Sea Voyage* (1622) and Suckling's *Goblins* (1667). This edition contains no textual or commentary notes.

261. Kennedy, Harlan. "Prospero's Flicks." *Film Comment* 28.1 (January-February 1992): 45–49.

Kennedy argues that *Tmp* is arguably "the most oft-adapted stagework in screen history" (45) because its characters span the full range of human possibilities, from the bestial Caliban to the godlike Prospero, and because of the appeal of the play's emphasis on forgiveness and regeneration. Focusing primarily on William Wellman's *Yellow Sky*, Fred McLeod Wilcox's *Forbidden Planet* (no. 268), Paul Mazursky's *Tempest* (1982), and Peter Greenaway's *Prospero's Books* (no. 259), Kennedy traces some of the ways in which each of these films selects from *Tmp* the concerns that are of greatest interest to a specific audience.

262. Lanier, Douglas. "Drowning the Book: *Prospero's Books* and the Textual Shakespeare." In *Shakespeare, Theory, and Performance*, ed. James C. Bulman, 187–209. London: Routledge, 1996.

Questioning the authority of the Shakespearean text as "regulatory guide" (188) for performance, Lanier explores the relation between cinema and text in several films, concentrating on Peter Greenaway's *Prospero's Books* (no. 259). Greenaway's translation of *Tmp*'s words and the play's sources into images, Lanier argues, stresses *Tmp*'s intertextuality and makes the text seem an imperfect record of a performance. John Gielgud's performance, Lanier adds, actually seems to create the text. The essay concludes by elucidating the cinematic means through which Prospero's Books stimulates thought concerning the relations among "the media that render performance capable of study" (204–5), including film, video, promptbooks, production notes, and Shakespearean text.

263. Mannoni, O[ctave]. *Prospero and Caliban: The Psychology of Colonization.* 2nd edition. Trans. Pamela Powesland. New York: Praeger, 1964. Repr., with foreword by Maurice Bloch, Ann Arbor: Univ. of Michigan Press, 1990.

Writing in the aftermath of a bloody anticolonial revolt in Madagascar, Mannoni attempts to explain the relations between colonial masters and the conquered population in terms of psychoanalytical concepts that he believes apply to all cultures. For Mannoni, colonizers suffer from an inferiority complex that leads to the desire for dominance, expressed as magic in *Tmp*; the colonized exist in a stage of evolution that entails a dependency complex, a need for parents that manifests itself in such practices as ancestor worship. When deprived of native forms of government, Mannoni believes, the colonized become dependent on the colonizers, who in turn exploit and thus betray them. This betrayal, he concludes, evokes the furious rebellion that we see in Caliban and that Mannoni witnessed in Madagascar. Mannoni argues that psychoanalytical interpretation of literary works such as *Tmp* and Daniel Defoe's *Robinson Crusoe* reveals deep truths about the psyche. Bloch's trenchant criticism of Mannoni's influential theories in the 1990 foreword (v–xx) points out that analysis of the Western literary tradition is no substitute for empirical study of Malagasy culture. Bloch credits Mannoni with recognizing that analysis of colonial experience must be central to studies of African cultures; with calling attention to the need for analysis of the psychology of the colonizers; and with a degree of self-criticism in his prefaces of 1956 and 1964. Yet he stresses that even Mannoni's analysis of the psychology of the colonizers is not based on sufficient empirical research. Mannoni provides a self-critical analysis of his earlier work in "The Decolonisation of Myself," *Race* (April 1966), repr. in *Clefs pour l'Imaginaire ou l'Autre Scène.* Paris: Seuil, 1969.

264. Novy, Marianne, ed. *Transforming Shakespeare: Contemporary Women's Re-Visions in Literature and Performance.* New York: St. Martin's Press, 1999.

This collection includes three items relating to *Tmp*. Linda Bamber's short story (no. 253) is annotated elsewhere in this volume. Diana Brydon (199–216) discusses Canadian writer Nancy Huston's *Plainsong* (1993) as a novel that "invokes *The Tempest* primarily to claim the power of art as magic to transcend differences and effect reconciliations" (213) among the descendants of colonizers and indigenous populations. Caroline Cakebread (217–35) interprets Marina Warner's *Indigo* (1992), a novel that responds to *Tmp* in the context of twentieth-century characters' struggles with the legacy of British imperialism. Novy's introduction (1–12) discusses the various purposes of "re-visioning" Shakespeare: understanding the complexities of the past; freeing oneself from patriarchal tradition; claiming Shakespeare as powerful cultural ally, sometimes as artist or cultural outsider. She then surveys briefly the history of women's responses to Shakespeare. Additional works on this subject include *Cross-Cultural Performances: Differences in Women's Re-Visions of Shakespeare*, ed. Marianne Novy (Urbana: Univ. of Illinois press, 1993); Novy, *Engaging with Shakespeare: Responses of George Eliot and Other Women Novelists* (Athens: Univ. of Georgia Press, 1994; Iowa City: Univ. of Iowa Press, 1998); and Peter Erickson, *Rewriting Shakespeare, Rewriting Ourselves* (Berkeley and Los Angeles: Univ. of California Press, 1991).

265. Porter, Laurence M. "Aimé Césaire's Reworking of Shakespeare: Anticolonialist Discourse in *Une Tempête*." *Comparative Literature Studies* 32 (1995): 360–81.

Porter acknowledges that the primary source for Caliban is probably the wild man figure of European literature, rather than the actual or imagined inhabitants of the New World, yet he also believes that Shakespeare's assumption of the essential superiority of Western civilization is easily appropriated by European colonialists. This article argues that *Une Tempête* (no. 256), Césaire's parody of *Tmp*, subverts the myth of European superiority by affirming in its characterization of Caliban the dignity of the language and the social and religious values of a conquered, non-European culture.

266. Summers, Montague, ed. *Shakespeare Adaptations: "The Tempest," "The Mock Tempest," and "King Lear."* 1922. Repr. New York: Benjamin Blom, 1966.

This volume includes John Dryden and William Davenant's *The Tempest, or The Enchanted Island* (performed 1667; pub. 1670); Thomas Duffett's *Mock Tempest, or the Enchanted Castle* (performed 1674; pub. 1675); and Nahum Tate's revision of *King Lear*. Summers' preface (xi–xv) discusses these works' publication history and notes that several early editors and H. H. Furness (no. 181) erroneously printed Thomas Shadwell's operatic version of *The Tempest* (1674) as though it were the original Dryden-Davenant work. The introduction (xvii–cviii) provides a history of Shakespearean production, adaptation, and burlesque in the Restoration and 18th century, with detailed accounts of the genesis, organization, and personnel of major theatrical companies. Textual and commentary notes follow the texts.

267. **Vaughan, Alden T., and Virginia Mason Vaughan.** *Shakespeare's Caliban: A Cultural History.* Cambridge: Cambridge Univ. Press, 1991.

This study begins with an inquiry into Shakespeare's sources and intentions in his creation of Caliban. It then discusses the history of interpretations, appropriations, and adaptations of *Tmp* as reflections of different values and ideologies. The introduction (chap. 1, 3–20) assesses the evidence concerning Caliban's appearance and analyzes his role as a foil to other characters. Part II, "Origins," explores (chap. 2, 23–55) possible etymological and historical connections between Caliban and cannibals, Caribs, gypsies, American Indians, Africans, and rebellious British commoners. The Vaughans then survey (chap. 3, 56–85) literary sources ranging from the *Aeneid* through the wild men and monsters of literature and pageantry. In part III, "Receptions," the Vaughans argue (chap. 4, 89–117) that the Restoration and 18th century emphasized the triumph of reason and authority over disorder, and any complexities in the subversive Caliban were therefore eliminated. They then discuss the Romantics' sympathy with Caliban, the Victorians' view of the character as Darwinian missing link, and the moral and psychological interests of the early 20th century. Chap. 5 (118–43) surveys treatments of Caliban as American Indian, from the racist views of some early critics through anti-colonialist readings. The Vaughans discuss Third-World appropriations of *Tmp* in chap. 6 (144–71), arguing that writers whose consciousness is Euro-centric use Caliban as a symbol of the Yankee imperialist, while those who seek non-European cultural roots see Caliban as an oppressed colonial subject. The Vaughans provide surveys of stage history (chap. 7, 172–98), screen history (chap. 8, 199–214), artists' renditions (chap. 9, 215–51), and modern poetic invocations (chap. 10, 252–70), finding a greater variety of responses among artists and poets than among literary critics. The Vaughans conclude (part IV, 273–84) that Shakespeare intended Caliban to symbolize "a general unruliness in society and in nature" (278), and they suggest the limitations of strictly political interpretations of this multifaceted character. Chaps. 5, 6, and 7 are expansions of the following articles: Virginia Mason Vaughan, " 'Something Rich and Strange': Caliban's Theatrical Metamorphoses," *SQ* 36 (1985): 390–405; Alden T. Vaughan, "Shakespeare's Indian: The Americanization of Caliban," *SQ* 39 (1988): 137–53; Alden T. Vaughan, "Caliban in the 'Third World': Shakespeare's Savage as Sociopolitical Symbol," *Massachusetts Review* 29 (1988): 289–313.

268. **Wilcox, Fred McLeod,** director. Nicholas Nayfack, producer. *Forbidden Planet.* Screenplay by Cyril Hume, based on a story by Irving Black and Allen Adler. Metro Goldwin Mayer, 1956.

Tmp is a major source of this film, which dramatizes the visit of a group of space travellers to an isolated planet occupied by Dr. Morbius (Walter Pidgeon), a mad scientist who in some ways resembles Prospero, and his daughter Altaira (Anne Francis), who appears to combine characteristics of both Miranda and Ariel. The planet is terrorized by a monster that emerges from Morbius's subconscious. Available from Facets Multimedia, The Writing Company, and elsewhere. For additional information and commentary, see nos. 24 (item 611), 94, 261, 272.

See also nos. 94, 185a, 205, 222a, 234, 238, 245, 248, 270, 271b, 272, 276, 277.

H. Pedagogy.

269. Peterson, Douglas L. "The Utopias of *The Tempest.*" In Hunt (no. 95), 139–45.

Peterson argues that teachers should distinguish between utopian visions that are escapist wish-fulfillments and those that affirm "exemplary ... modes of conduct" as "ideal solutions to real problems" (142). In the first category are the utopia envisioned by Gonzalo in 2.1 and the wedding masque performed in act 4; in the latter category, Peterson suggests, is *Tmp* itself. For Peterson, the play affirms the Renaissance humanists' belief in the possibility of learning from the past and of striving—despite our awareness of human fallibility—to re-create oneself and human society through virtues such as forgiveness. See also no. 80.

See also no. 95.

I. Collections.

270. Bloom, Harold, ed. *Caliban.* Major Literary Characters. New York: Chelsea House, 1992.

This anthology reprints the following items annotated elsewhere in this volume: Skura (no. 239); Vaughan, "Caliban's Theatrical Metamorphoses" (revised in no. 267); and an excerpt from Smith (no. 212), retitled as "Caliban." It also contains John W. Draper's essay on Caliban's physical appearance and his possible origins (89–94); Barbara Melchiori's discussion (95–108) of Browning's reflections upon the evolution of theology in "Caliban upon Setebos" (no. 254); Mike Frank's argument that nature is providential in Shakespeare's tragedies but not in *Tmp* and that Prospero's subjugation of Caliban symbolizes the necessary domination of brute nature by human civilization (109–23); Jacqueline E. M. Latham's "*The Tempest* and *King James's Daemonologie*" (151–58); Lucy S. and John McDiarmid's analysis of Auden's response to *Tmp* in "The Sea and the

Mirror" (159–78); and G. Wilson Knight's argument (179–91) that Caliban's style of speech and his sensitivity to both nature and the supernatural link him with "the Red Men of North America" (187). Kenneth Maclean (207–20) discusses Shakespeare's and Browning's characterization of Caliban in relation to the wild man as Jungian "shadow," an embodiment of subconscious fears of death. (See no. 254.) Bloom also includes 29 brief excerpts from criticism ranging from Dryden through the 20th century, including Frye (no. 62), Girard (no. 63), Kermode's Arden introduction (no. 182), Orgel (no. 184), Fiedler (no. 194), Greenblatt (no. 196), and Berger (no. 219). Bloom's essay on "The Analysis of Character" (ix–xiv) rejects poststructuralist theories of textuality and argues that as readers we search for realistic characters who experience our own most profound desires and fears. (See Bloom's development of these arguments in no. 53.) The introduction (1–4) criticizes readings of *Tmp* that stress only colonialist ideology and asserts that the story of Prospero and Caliban resembles a tragic father-son relationship in which love has failed. Bloom includes a bibliography (251–54) and an index (257–62), and, for longer selections, authors' original bibliographical notes.

271. Bloom, Harold, ed. *William Shakespeare's "The Tempest."* Modern Critical Interpretations. New York: Chelsea House, 1988.

This anthology reprints the following items annotated elsewhere in this volume: Brown (no. 190), Berger (no. 219), Orgel (no. 238) and excerpts from Greenblatt (no. 196), and Traister (no. 240). James P. Driscoll (85–98) argues that Prospero develops a combination of skepticism and faith that enables him to hope for a better world while eschewing metaphysical certainties and accepting tragedy and death. (For commentary, see no. 238a.) Marjorie Garber (43–63) provides structuralist analysis of repetitions and juxtapositions in *Tmp*; Garber also discusses Prospero as a Daedalus figure whose art teaches us to accept human nature as neither fully godlike nor entirely bestial. Julian Patrick (69–84) discusses the play's structure in relation to audience-response criticism. Bloom includes a bibliography (157–62) and index (165–71), but he eliminates the authors' original bibliographical notes.

271a. Graff, Gerald, and James Phelan, eds. *William Shakespeare's "The Tempest": A Case Study in Critical Controversy.* Boston and New York: Bedford/St. Martin's, 2000.

Part 1 of this book consists of a brief biography of Shakespeare (3–9) and a reprint of David Bevington's edition of *Tmp* (no. 1). Part 2 begins with the editors' argument (91–108) in favor of "learning by controversy" (92) as a method that enables students to make their own critical judgments.

Graff and Phelan then reprint (109–15) opposing essays by George Will and
Stephen Greenblatt on the value of ideological criticism of literature. "Sources
and Contexts" (116–72) provides extracts from Montaigne's "Of the Can-
nibals," Strachey's *True Reportory of the Wracke and Redemption of Sir
Thomas Gates*, Jourdain's *Discovery of the Bermudas*, Hakluyt's "Reasons
for Colonization," and Bartolomé de Las Casas's letter to King Philip of
Spain protesting the mistreatment of the inhabitants of the New World.
This section concludes with Ronald Takaki's interpretation of *Tmp* in the
context of early modern Europeans' attitudes toward American Indians.
The volume then reprints the following items annotated elsewhere in this
volume: Barker and Hulme (no. 187), Brown (no. 190), Kastan (no. 200),
Brower (no. 221), Skura (no. 239), and extracts from Kermode (no. 70),
Loomba (no. 205), and Césaire (no. 256). Deborah Willis (256–68) affirms
political analysis but criticizes the tendency of some critics (notably
Brown, no. 190) to oversimplify *Tmp* so that it "vanishes almost completely
into the 'domain' of colonialist discourse" (258). Ann Thompson (337–47)
assesses recent psychoanalytical and colonialist interpretation of *Tmp* and
asks (but does not answer) the question, "Must a feminist reading necessarily be a negative one?" (347). The editors' introductions to groups of
essays provide summaries of the arguments and commentary on rival theoretical positions.

271b. Hulme, Peter, and William H. Sherman, eds. *"The Tempest" and
Its Travels.* London: Reaktion; Philadelphia: Univ. of Pennsylvania Press,
2000.

This collection organizes nineteen essays into three categories. The first,
"Local Knowledge," focuses upon historical contexts of *Tmp*'s original composition and early performances. Crystal Bartlovich (13–26) argues that *Tmp*
reflects early modern anxieties concerning aliens in an increasingly cosmo-
politan London. Barbara Mowat (27–36) explores the literary effects of
the play's intertextuality; she emphasizes that the play's evocation of such
works as *The Aeneid* underscores its relation to imperialism, while the
Biblical allusions in 4.1.146–63 remind us of the transitory nature of em-
pires and civilizations. Elizabeth Fowler (37–40) discusses *Tmp*'s use of
the "ship of state" topos and concludes that the play's exploration of
questions concerning the "limits, duties and sources of authority" (39) is
open-ended. Christy Anderson (41–47) relates the play's aesthetic to early
modern interest in wonderful machinery. Alden T. Vaughan (48–59) nar-
rates the stories of several American Indians who might have served as
sources for Trinculo and Stephano's references to a "dead Indian" (2.2.33)
and "men of Inde" (2.2.58). Joseph Roach (60–70) discusses restoration adaptations of *Tmp* by John Dryden and William Davenant, Thomas Shadwell,

and Thomas Duffett as central to the period's conception of the stage as an enchanted island and realm of innocence to which the audience may enjoy vicarious travel. Section 2, "European and Mediterranean Crossroads," includes essays on political issues associated with the play's Mediterranean setting. Robin Kirkpatrick's "The Italy of The Tempest" is annotated elsewhere in this volume (no. 201a). Marina Warner (97–113) argues that *Tmp* contrasts Sycorax's feminine, transformative, and erotic witchcraft with Prospero's patriarchal, Christian magic that strives for fixed identities. Donna B. Hamilton (114–20) discusses *Tmp*'s responses to political uses of *The Aeneid*; she concludes that Prospero's renunciation of magic suggests the play's opposition to royal absolutism. Andrew Hess (121–30) discusses *Tmp*'s implicit critique of alliance with Islamic cultures and its affirmation of European values, including a vision of "a human ability to reject the past and determine the future" (130). Jerry Brotton (131–37) discusses 16th-century representations of Tunis in depictions of "magical but dangerous" (137) voyages. Roland Greene (138–45) argues that "insularity" stands for "a distinctively partial knowledge that counters the totalities of institutions and regimes" (138); he concludes that Prospero brings the Europeans back into "an inflected version of the [geographical and ideological] world they started from" (145). As transition to section 3, the editors provide brief accounts (147–67) of performances of the following offshoots of *Tmp*: Aimé Césaire's *Une Tempête* (no. 256); Raquel Carriô and Flora Lauten's *Otra Tempestad*; and Terra Nova Theatre Institute's *Tempest(s)*. The final section includes essays on *Tmp*'s relation to the Americas. John Gillies (180–200) explores the play's complex and self-reflexive relation to the multiple symbolic meanings of "the new world"; he concludes that in *Tmp* "the ambition to raise human nature to some prelapsarian yet millennial status is exposed as utopian," yet "the dream of renewal ... is [nonetheless] irreversible" (200). Patricia Seed (202–11) discusses both early modern laws concerning colonists' rights of ownership and the "increasingly masculine character of inheritance rights in England" (202) as a context for *Tmp*'s refutation of Caliban's claim to ownership of the island. Gordon Brotherston (212–19) surveys the responses to *Tmp* in Latin America. Peter Hulme (220–35) discusses George Lamming's *The Pleasures of Exile* (1960) as an interpretation of *Tmp* illuminating "the psychological effects of colonialism, not just on Caliban ... but also on Prospero" (228). Lucy Rix (236–49) discusses Aimé Césaire's analysis of the psychology of race and class in postcolonial Martinique in *Une Tempête* (no. 256). Martha Nell Smith (250–56) discusses H. D.'s transformation of Claribel from peripheral character to strong, central figure in *By Avon River*, and Smith quotes H. D.'s poem "The Tempest." David Dabydeen (257–63) argues that William Hogarth's *A Scene from "The Tempest"* implies sympathy with Caliban and an ambivalent representation of Ferdinand and Miranda. Dabydeen's poem "Miranda," based on the slave's fantasy of love, follows. *The Envoy* (265–68) includes two poems by Merle Collins, prefaced by the author, on the "double [linguistic and cultural] inheritance" of the colonized.

272. Lie, Nadia, and Theo D'haen, eds. *Constellation Caliban: Figurations of a Character.* Amsterdam: Editions Rodopi, 1997.

   This collection includes 17 essays. Dirk Delabastita (1–22) and Paul Franssen (23–42) survey interpretations of Caliban. Delabastita assesses them in the context of theories of intertextuality; Franssen concludes that *Tmp* itself suggests that "the Other can never be completely known" and that characters' interpretations of Caliban within the play are "mere self-serving constructions" (40). Barbara Baert (43–59) places Caliban within the iconography of the wild man as "the reverse of all that is human" (46). Drawing on works by Greenblatt (including nos. 196 and 197), Jürgen Pieters (61–79) discusses *Tmp*'s analysis of the demarcation between self and other. The remaining essays discuss works written in response to Shakespeare's Caliban: Koenraad Geldof (81–112) on Ernest Renan's *Caliban* (1878) and Jean Guéhenno's *Caliban parle* (1962), *Caliban et Prospero* (1969), and other works; Ortwin de Graef (113–43) on Browning's "Caliban upon Setebos" (no. 254); Maarten van Delden (145–61) on Uruguayan essayist José Enrique Rodó's *Ariel* (1900); Bart Philipsen and Georgi Verbeeck (163–83) on Arnold Zweig's analysis of antisemitism in *Caliban or Politics and Passions* (1927); Kristine Vanden Berghe (185–98) on Argentinian Marxist Aníbal Ponce's "Ariel or the Agony of a Stubborn Illusion" (1935); Herman Servotte (198–210) on W. H. Auden's "The Sea and the Mirror" (no. 252); Tim Youngs (211–29) on Fred McLeod Wilcox's film, *Forbidden Planet* (no. 268); A. James Arnold (231–44) on postcolonial literature of the Caribbean since the 1960s, principally Aimé Césaire (no. 256) and Edward Braithwaite; Nadia Lie (245–70) on Cuban writer Roberto Fernández Retamar's "Calibán" (1971) and subsequent cultural/political essays; Chantal Zabus and Kevin A. Dwyer (271–89) on Jarman's *Tempest* (no. 249) and Greenaway's *Prospero's Books* (no. 259); Hedwig Schwall (291–311) on John Banville's novel *Ghosts* (1993); and Theo D'haen (313–31) on Rachel Ingalls's *Mrs. Caliban* (1982) and Tad Williams's *Caliban's Hour* (1994). The volume concludes with C. C. Barfoot's poem, "The Tempest Transposed or Caliban on the Moors" (333–41). Many of the contributors respond to Vaughan and Vaughan (no. 267).

273. Maquerlot, Jean-Pierre, and Michèle Willems, eds. *Travel and Drama* *in Shakespeare's Time.* Cambridge: Cambridge Univ. Press, 1996.

This collection includes three essays on *Tmp*. Andrew Gurr (193–208) suggests that seeing Prospero, Ariel, and Caliban as, respectively, a London patriarch and his industrious and idle apprentices is as apposite to the play as is New World colonization. Leo Salingar discusses (209–21) *Tmp*'s allusions to travellers' tales in the context of the play's naturalization of the marvelous. Gunter Walch (223–38) argues that *Tmp*'s metatheatricality (i.e., its reflection on its own artistic methods and its relation to Shakespeare's previous plays) enhances its "productive openness" (228) to interpretation.

274. Palmer, D. J., ed. Shakespeare, *"The Tempest": A Casebook.* London: Macmillan, 1969. Repr. Nashville: Aurora, 1970.

Part 1 of this collection (27–105) includes excerpts from the Dryden-Davenant *Tmp* (see nos. 260, 266), Auden's "The Sea and the Mirror" (no. 252), and criticism by John Dryden, Nicholas Rowe, Joseph Warton, Samuel Johnson, S. T. Coleridge, William Hazlitt, Edward Dowden, and Henry James. Part 2 (109–258) includes the following items annotated elsewhere in this volume: Brower (no. 221), Kott (no. 232), and excerpts from Knight (no. 71), Tillyard (no. 84), and Kermode (no. 182). Additional selections include J. Middleton Murry's interpretation (109–21) of Prospero as an artist who seeks to reform nature; John P. Cutts's analysis (196–211) of the play's use of music in relation to themes of cosmic harmony and discord; Frank Davidson's reading (212–31) based on Renaissance conceptions of order and the importance of reason controlling passion; and Rose Zimbardo's argument (232–43) that the central concern of *Tmp* is Prospero's imperfect effort to impose order upon chaos through art. Palmer's introduction (11–24) discusses date; sources; and the play's reception history. Palmer celebrates *Tmp*'s blend of "realism and fantasy" (16).

275. Smith, Hallett, ed. *Twentieth-Century Interpretations of "The Tempest": A Collection of Critical Essays.* Englewood Cliffs, N.J.: Prentice-Hall, 1969.

This collection includes Knight's "Myth and Miracle" (in no. 71) and excerpts from Kermode (no. 182) and Nuttall (no. 236). It also includes interpretations by Arthur Quiller-Couch, E. E. Stoll, John Dover Wilson, Theodore Spencer, Bonamy Dobrée, Northrop Frye, C. J. Sisson (in no. 106), and Don Cameron Allen. The section entitled "View Points" contains brief excerpts of commentary by A. C. Bradley, Lytton Strachey, Clifford Leech, John Wain, and Harry Levin. Smith's introduction (1–11) emphasizes *Tmp*'s aesthetic excellence, including the quality of the verse and the effectiveness of its masque-like spectacle, and expresses skepticism concerning allegorical and philosophical interpretations.

276. Vaughan, Virginia Mason, and Alden T. Vaughan. *Critical Essays on Shakespeare's "The Tempest."* New York: G. K. Hall; London: Prentice Hall International, 1998.

This collection reprints the following items annotated elsewhere in this volume: Mowat (no. 208), McDonald (no. 217), Skura (no. 239), and excerpts from Bate (no. 28) and Warren (no. 92). It also includes Donna Hamilton's "Defiguring Virgil in *The Tempest*" (17–38), an essay subsequently revised as part of no. 198; David Kastan's " 'The Duke of Milan and His Brave Son': Dynastic Politics in *The Tempest*," revised as no. 200; and Alden T. Vaughan's "Caliban in the 'Third World' " (247–66), revised as chap. 7 of no. 267. Keith Sturgess (107–29) argues that what we know of *Tmp*'s original staging at Blackfriars underscores the play's dream-like and delicate aesthetic effects. Trevor R. Griffths (130–51) analyzes discussions of race, Darwinism, and colonialism in *Tmp*'s critical and performance history. Ann Thompson (234–43) assesses recent psychoanalytical and colonialist interpretation of *Tmp* and asks (but does not answer) the question, "Must a feminist reading necessarily be a negative one?" (242). The Vaughans' introduction (1–14) briefly surveys *Tmp*'s reception history and influence.

277. Wells, Stanley, ed. *Shakespeare Survey* 43 (for 1990).

This issue of *Shakespeare Survey* contains a cluster of essays on *Tmp* and its influence. The essay by Russ McDonald (no. 217) is annotated elsewhere in this volume. Kurt Tetzeli von Rosador (1–13) discusses the rival claims of magicians and monarchs to "transcendental legitimation" (2) of their power in Renaissance drama, concluding that *Tmp* consigns the magicians' claims to the realm of theatrical illusion. James Black (29–41) discusses the centrality of betrothal and marriage to *Tmp*'s multiple plots, and he stresses the necessity of forgiveness as prerequisite to the return to Milan. Matthew H. Wikander (91–98) argues that the Dryden-Davenant *Tmp* affects an innocence it does not fully possess in its semi-concealed analysis of "the limitations of Stuart absolutist ideology" (98). Michael Dobson (99–107) analyzes the role of patriarchal and imperialist ideologies in shaping appropriations of *Tmp* from 1700 to 1800. Inga-Stina Ewbank (109–19) discusses the contrasting responses of August Strindberg, Henrik Ibsen, and Isak Dinesen to *Tmp*, suggesting that the value of the play lies in part in its ability to evoke powerful personal responses. Martin Scofield (121–29) explores *Tmp*'s influence on T. S. Eliot, suggesting that a poet's work may be a compound of literary influence, personal experience, and spiritual quest. Interestingly, this volume juxtaposes essays that stress ideological analysis with those that emphasize traditional aesthetics.

277a. White, R. S., ed. *The Tempest.* New Casebooks. New York: St. Martin's Press, 1999.

This collection reprints the following items annotated elsewhere in this volume: Barker and Hulme (no. 187), Norbrook (no. 235), Orgel (no. 238), and extracts from Nevo (no. 77), Gillies (no. 195), Greenblatt (no. 197), and Loomba (no. 205). Terence Hawkes (49–74) analyzes cultural assumptions concerning master-servant and landlord-tenant relations in *Tmp*. Annabel Patterson (123–34) questions the "assumption ... that Shakespeare's play was fully complicit in a mythology of benevolent colonialism" (124) or other forms of authoritarian political ideology. Ann Thompson (155–66) assesses recent psychoanalytical and colonialist interpretation of *Tmp* and asks (but does not answer) the question, "Must a feminist reading necessarily be a negative one?" (242). The introduction (1–14) surveys the history of adaptation and revision of *Tmp* in "new cultural contexts down the centuries" (2).

278. Wood, Nigel, ed. *The Tempest.* Theory in Practice. Buckingham, England: Open Univ. Press, 1995.

This collection explores the implications of different literary theories for interpretation of *Tmp*. The essays by Felperin (no. 224) and Turner (no. 241) are annotated elsewhere in this volume. Charles Frey (67–96) recommends an aesthetic experience that is burdened as little as possible by abstract theory; his analysis of *Tmp* emphasizes the power of "Shakespeare's relentlessly somatic imagination" (84) to evoke physical and emotional responses. Richard P. Wheeler (127–64) argues that a psychoanalytical approach can illuminate recurrent motifs in *Tmp* and the Shakespeare canon, focusing upon "what the individual brings to the encounter with history, out of which the subject is constituted" (160). Wood's introduction (1–28) surveys *Tmp*'s critical history; discusses its theatrical and political contexts; and considers ways that the play complicates our understanding of Prospero's power and authority. Wood provides brief theoretical introductions for each essay; following each contribution is a question-and-answer supplement in which Wood and the contributor discuss general theoretical issues.

J. Bibliographies.

See nos. 95, 110, 111, 112, 113, 181, 182, 183, 184, 222, 222a.

INDEX I: AUTHORS, EDITORS, DIRECTORS, AND PRODUCERS (SECTIONS II–V)

Index I includes, in addition to scholarly authors and editors, the primary entries for authors of creative works that are influenced by *Cym*, *WT*, and *Tmp* and are annotated in this volume. Commentary on creative works is included (also under authors' names) in Index II. Similarly, Index I includes entries for film versions and adaptations. Commentary on films, adaptations, and stage productions is included in Index II. Citations are to item number.

INDEX II: SUBJECTS
(FOR SECTIONS II–V)

The following indexes the contents of annotations in sections II, III, IV, and V. Texts (including Shakespeare's works but excluding *Cym*, *WT*, and *Tmp*) are listed under the author's names. *Cym*, *WT*, and *Tmp* are listed in the index only when a specific act and scene have been cited or are discussed; act, scene, and line numbers (if relevant) are given sequentially under each play. Characters are also listed individually. Citations are to item number.

CYMBELINE, THE WINTER'S TALE, AND THE TEMPEST

Shakespeare's late plays present rich challenges to both reader and playgoer, challenges which are impressively met in this seventh volume of the Pegasus Shakespeare Bibliographies. While the volume as a whole follows the scheme of the whole series (described on the next page), with the careful selection of entries, insistence on high quality or significant influence, full and useful annotations, detailed indexes, etc., this volume has two unusual features: A substantial section deals with the late plays as a group, and in each of the three sections devoted to the individual plays, Professor Mebane includes entries on adaptations and video and film versions.

JOHN S. MEBANE, the editor of this volume, is Professor of English and Director of the Honors Program at the University of Alabama, Huntsville. He is the author of *Renaissance Magic and the Return of the Golden Age: The Occult Tradition and Marlowe, Jonson, and Shakespeare*, and of numerous articles in *Shakespeare Yearbook*, *Renaissance Drama*, *College English*, *South Atlantic Review*, *Texas Studies in Literature and Language*, and other journals.

PEGASUS SHAKESPEARE BIBLIOGRAPHIES

The Pegasus Shakespeare Bibliographies — to total 12 volumes — provide handy and authoritative guides to Shakespeare scholarship and criticism. They are prepared for faculty and students in universities and colleges, as well as in high schools. Edited by leading scholar/teachers of Shakespeare, each volume is organized for ease of use. There are approximately 250 entries per volume of 160 pages; these have been selected as the best and most useful books and essays. The editors include only work of high quality or significant influence; partisanship is carefully avoided.

Most importantly, the annotations are full and helpful. The editors describe each item clearly so that a reader can quickly tell whether a particular essay or book would be useful. Cross-references and rich indexes complement the convenient organization of entries. So, with minimal effort, a reader will be able to find the right critical or scholarly resources. Additionally, the full annotations provide a good grasp of Shakespeare criticism and scholarship.

THE BOOKS ARE EMINENTLY USER-FRIENDLY,

AND THE LOW PRICE ($9.95 PER VOLUME) IS FANTASTIC!

Each volume includes most or all of the following sections:

Editions and Reference Works
Authorship, Dating, Textual Studies
Influences; Sources; Historical and Intellectual Backgrounds
Language and Linguistics
Criticism
Stage History and Performance Criticism
Reception History
Adaptations
Teaching and Collections of Essays
Bibliographies
Author & Subject Indexes

Send orders to our distributor—
Cornell University Press Services
750 Cascadilla Street
PO Box 6525
Ithaca, New York 14851
Email: orderbook@cupserv.org

PEGASUS SHAKESPEARE BIBLIOGRAPHIES

Volumes in Print

Love's Labor's Lost, A Midsummer Night's Dream, and The Merchant of Venice. Ed. Clifford Chalmers Huffman (1995) 0–86698–177–2

King Lear and Macbeth. Ed. Rebecca W. Bushnell (1996) 1–889818–00–3

Shakespeare and the Renaissance Stage to 1616 / Shakespearean Stage History 1616 to 1998. Ed. Hugh Macrae Richmond (1999) 1–889818–22–4

Richard II, 1 and 2 Henry IV, and Henry V. Ed. Joseph Candido (1998) 1–889818–10–0

Hamlet. Ed. Michael E. Mooney (1999) 1–889818–21–6

The Rape of Lucrece, Titus Andronicus, Julius Caesar, Antony and Cleopatra, and Coriolanus. Ed. Clifford Chalmers Huffman and John W. Velz (2002) 1–889818–30–5

Cymbeline, The Winter's Tale, and The Tempest. Ed. John S. Mebane (2002) 1–889818–31–3

Shakespeare: Life, Language & Linguistics, Textual Studies, and The Canon. Ed. Michael Warren (2002) 1–889818–34–8

As You Like It, Much Ado About Nothing, and Twelfth Night, or What You Will. Ed. Marilyn L. Williamson (2003) 1–889818–35–6

Volumes in Preparation

Jean Howard on Shakespeare criticism and literary theory

Jill Levenson on *Romeo and Juliet* and *Othello*

Barbara Traister on *Troilus and Cressida, Measure for Measure*, and *All's Well That Ends Well*

Price for each volume: $9.95.
Discounts for standing orders.

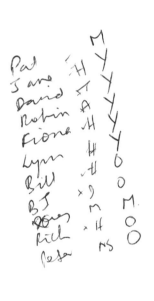

Pat   M
Jane   H   Y
David   A   Y
Robin   A   Y
Fiona   H   Y
Lynn   H   Y
Bill   H   O
BJ   D   O
Doug   M   M
Rich   H   O
Peter   NS   O